D1339085

RHIGAS VELESTINLIS

THE PROTO-MARTYR
OF THE
GREEK REVOLUTION

RHIGAS VELESTINLIS

THE PROTO-MARTYR
OF THE
GREEK REVOLUTION

BY

C. M. WOODHOUSE

*All historical experience confirms that men
might not achieve the possible if they had not,
time and again, reached out for the impossible.*
Max Weber

DENISE HARVEY (PUBLISHER) • LIMNI, EVIA, GREECE

First published by Denise Harvey (Publisher)
340 05 Limni, Evia, Greece

ISBN 960-7120-08-6 *cloth*
ISBN 960-7120-09-4 *paper*

Rhigas Velestinlis
The Proto-Martyr of the Greek Revolution
is the fourteenth publication in
THE ROMIOSYNI SERIES

Dedicated to the memory of
LEANDROS VRANOUSIS
(1921–1993)
a learned authority on the
life of Rhigas
and a comrade in arms in a later
war of national liberation
1941–1944

ACKNOWLEDGEMENTS

I would like to thank Euthymia Provata for her diligent help in searching out illustrative material for this volume, Dr Dimitrios Karamberopoulos, President of the 'Pherai – Velestino – Rhigas' Scientific Research Society, who generously lent material from his archives, and the University of Thessaly for permission to reproduce the wall-painting of Rhigas by Thanasis Pagonis.

CONTENTS

Rhigas Pheraios by Thanasis Pagonis; wall-painting from the Saravani house in Drakia, Pelion, c. 1870 (courtesy of the University of Thessaly).

PREFACE

WHEN Louis XVI was told that the Bastille had fallen to a Parisian mob on 14 July 1789, he commented: 'This is a great revolt.' His informant, the Duc de Liancourt, replied: 'No, Sir: it is a great revolution!' The distinction was correctly made, and very important.

A revolt is a violent upsurge of discontent, usually localised, unplanned and short-lived. If it fails, things go on as before, only worse. If it succeeds, superficial reforms follow, which may also be short-lived. A revolution normally is also violent, though not localised or unplanned, except in its early stages; but it is also much more. If it fails, it may still leave behind it the seeds of future success. If it succeeds, its consequences are neither superficial nor short-lived, but radical, permanent, and all-embracing. It transforms society culturally, educationally and morally. It alters the course of history and the maps of continents. It is an ideological as well as a political event. Obvious examples are the American Revolution of 1776 and the French Revolution of 1789.

By these definitions, the Greeks launched innumerable revolts against the Ottoman Empire between 1453 and 1821; and in the latter year they started a revolution which was ultimately successful. Their only other attempt at a revolution, in the sense defined, occurred a quarter of a century earlier. Little is known of it outside Greece, because it failed. But in some ways it is not less interesting than the revolution which succeeded, because it was more ideological as well as more tragic. It makes, too, a more concentrated drama, with a single hero worthy of Sophocles: a commanding figure with a fatal weakness; a poet, scholar and visionary; a merchant, patriot and revolutionary, whose trust and confidence went too far, and were betrayed.

The life and death of Rhigas Velestinlis, known as the 'proto-martyr' of the Greek struggle for independence, have naturally provided favourite themes for Greek historians, poets and writers. His story has also drawn the attention of some French writers, because of his attachment to the Enlightenment and to revolutionary France; and also of German writers, because of the Austrian role in the last act of his tragedy. In English little has been written about him. British and American philhellenes in the nineteenth century concentrated on the revolution of 1821, in which a number of them took part. Rhigas earned no more than a passing reference in the works of Thomas Gordon, Martin Leake or George Finlay.

The only biography of Rhigas in English was written by Mrs B. E. Edmonds, and published in 1890. Her timing was unlucky, because it was in that year that Professor Émile Legrand found in the Austrian state archives at Vienna the files containing the interrogation reports on Rhigas and his associates, together with related minutes and correspondence. These documents were published in 1892, with a Greek translation by Professor S. Lambros. Thus Rhigas was brought for the first time within the scope of documented history. Further discoveries in the Austrian archives were made by Professor K. Amantos (1930), Professor P. K. Enepekidis (1955), and other Greek scholars. More data, though nothing of equal importance, have been found elsewhere. Almost all the scholarly work on Rhigas's life and times has been the work of Greek scholars, in contrast with the more widely international contributions on the revolution of 1821 and later Greek history.

For the time being at least the process of extracting new material has slowed down almost to a halt. Although major new discoveries cannot be excluded, the time seems ripe for a considered assessment of his role in English. It can at least be more securely based than it could a century ago. At a personal level, it also seems to me an obligation to offer some amends for the sad fact that at the time of the first abortive struggle for Greek independence, in contrast with that of 1821, England not only made no contribution to the cause but was rightly seen as the ally of Greece's enemies.

A fresh attempt to examine his role in the history of south-east Europe therefore needs no apology. The material available is now enormous. Practically none of it is in English; most of it is in

Greek; but I do not assume any knowledge on the part of the reader of the language in this work. All quotations from Greek are translated. Occasional Greek words are transliterated; so are the titles of books and articles. Names which are familiar in English are given in their English form, except where a change of initial makes them almost unrecognisable. But perfect consistency is unattainable between two languages which have been exchanging vocabulary for centuries.

Two more minor points need to be made about transliteration. Some Greek scholars still use in their prefaces the classical numerals, derived from the Greek alphabet, for page numbers. In citing such passages, to avoid using Greek type which may be difficult to interpret, I have converted all such figures into the Roman numerals (i, ii, iii, etc.) which are more familiar to English readers. Secondly, in transliterating Turkish words, I have preferred the old phonetic system which was in use before the adoption of the Latinised alphabet in 1928, since it is not always clear in the latter how certain consonants are to be pronounced.

I

A YOUTH IN BONDAGE

THE life of Rhigas of Velestino begins and ends in legend. During his first thirty years—three-quarters of his life— very few dates are known with certainty. Even the date of his birth was a matter of conjecture, over a wide range of uncertainty, until the discovery in the Austrian state archives of a document dated 3 April 1798, in which his age was given as 40.[1] Since then it has been generally assumed that he was born in 1757, though it might have been early in 1758. From that point the stages of his life can be charted in outline, but there are no more precise dates until he is more or less positively identified at Bucharest in 1786.

As he adopted the surname Velestinlis, his place of birth is not in doubt. Velestino was a village in Thessaly, now a small town, close to Mount Pelion and the port of Volos. The ancient site nearby was Pherai, famous in mythology as the home of Admetus, the ignoble husband of the heroic Alcestis, and infamous in history as the capital of the tyrant Jason in the fourth century BC. In consequence Rhigas was sometimes called Pheraios instead of Velestinlis, though never by himself.

The name Rhigas, which stands in Greek for the King (*Rex*) in chess and playing cards, was also adoptive. Why he chose it is a mystery: no doubt he liked contributing to his own legend. He also called himself Antonios Zagoraios at one time, Zagora being another village in Mount Pelion where he spent part of his schooldays. Antonios was in fact his baptismal name; and it was as 'Antoine Rigas Villestindis [*sic*] of Zagora' that he became known to the French Consul at Trieste in 1797.[2] But his patronymic was another mystery until the present century. That it was in fact Kyritzis was only established when a book which had once belonged to him was found with the fly-leaf inscribed: Rhiga Kyritzi Velestinli.[3]

Kyritzis was evidently his father's proper name, not in his case a patronymic, since in the villages surnames in the modern sense were not in common use.[4] His mother's name was Maria. The

1

family is variously said to have been of Vlach, Albanian, Bulgarian, Slavonic or Levitical origin, but there is no doubt that Greek was their native language.[5] There was also a daughter, Asimo, and another son, Constantine (Kostis), who is said to have taken part in the early fighting of the War of Independence in 1821.[6] Most of what is known of Rhigas's childhood is due to the reminiscences of elderly peasants at Velestino and nearby (none of whom could have been alive when he lived there), which were compiled in 1885 with the help of a local schoolmaster.[7] They carry their own unmistakable quota of legend.

The father was a man of substance in one of the most prosperous areas of Greece under Ottoman Turkish rule. He is said to have owned three inns, a shop, a tannery, a dye-works and a weaving-shop, employing in all more than forty Greeks, and even some Turks. Industry and trade were occupations despised by the Turks, and left mainly in the hands of Greeks and other subject peoples. Thessaly particularly flourished on this indifference of its rulers, and Velestino was not exceptional. Forty miles further north, on the slopes of Mount Ossa, stood the village of Ambelakia, which in the eighteenth century was perhaps the richest community in Greece.[8] Most of its rivals in wealth were also in northern Greece (Thessaly, Macedonia and Epiros), apart from the mercantile islands and a few harbours such as Galaxidi on the Gulf of Corinth.

Kyritzis could afford to give his son an excellent education. Legend has it that the Turks systematically suppressed Greek education; but apart from occasional bouts of intolerance, their attitude was merely one of indifference. Good schools were established in many Greek communities throughout the Ottoman Empire, but again especially in northern Greece. Rhigas was taught to read and write by a village priest at home in Velestino, and then sent away to school first at Zagora, on the eastern side of Mount Pelion, and afterwards at Ambelakia on Mount Ossa. He was well taught, and took full advantage of it.

The cost of such advantages was a long absence from home during his boyhood. But indirect clues, however slight, show that these separations did not cloud his early years. He remained devoted to his family. When he grew up, loyalty to his father was to be the prime cause of his flight from home. After his father's

2

death, he brought his mother out of Thessaly to live with him at Bucharest. He also had his brother, Kostis, with him there, and paid the young man's debts.[9] His first chosen pseudonym, 'Antonios of Zagora', evidently recalled his schooldays on Mount Pelion. He was not unhappy, then, while he was away from home. It was a normal experience, since few villages were large enough to accommodate an adequate school. He must have lodged, as was customary, either with relatives or with close friends of the family.

Incidental details about the schools at Zagora and Ambelakia give clues to the special influence they had on Rhigas's education. The school at Zagora had a good library, thanks to the generosity of locally born Greeks who had prospered abroad. In particular, a merchant at Amsterdam, Ioannis Pringos, sent a collection of geographical works and atlases.[10] These provided the first stimulus to Rhigas's life-long fascination with cartography. At Ambelakia, the commercial atmosphere would naturally also have given an extra-mural stimulus to his interest in trade and manufacture.

His schooldays certainly laid the foundations of his conviction that education was the first essential for the Greek people if they were ever to become free. In his eyes, education was all-inclusive: it comprised history, languages, mathematics, the natural sciences; and it must be simultaneously academic, moral and philosophical. For a Greek eager to improve his mind, there could be no substitute for the classics in his own language. At what age his devotion to them began can only be conjectured, but his knowledge of them was undoubtedly both wide and deep.

The one surviving book which bears his signature on the flyleaf is a volume, published at Basle in 1561, which contains Proclus' *De sphaera*, Cleomedes' *De mundo*, Aratus' *Phaenomena*, Dionysius Afer's *Descriptio orbis habitabilis*, and J. Honter's *De cosmographiae rudimentis*.[11] This is a revealing sample, for such works are not light literature. They would be studied only by a man whose classical and scientific education had begun early and remained thorough.

But Rhigas learned something else in the course of his education: to respect and cherish, and not to despise, the spoken language of his provincial contemporaries. This language is known by various names: Romaic, demotic, 'spoken Greek', or the 'sim-

3

ple dialect'. Rhigas was among the first to use it as a literary language, and even to insist that it should become the official language of Greece. In later years he argued that, although it was desirable for the Greeks to learn their classical language (which he called Hellenic in contrast with demotic), the time for that to become universal would only come when they were free. While they were 'under the rod of Hassan and Mehmed', the dialect familiar to them from childhood must be used to enlighten them. The time was not yet ripe, though one day it would be, for them to 'converse with Homers and Thucydideses'.[12] These were the words of a deeply convinced educationalist, who must have formed his point of view early in life. The first biographer who knew Rhigas personally confirms that this was so by the respect with which he records the names of the schoolmasters in Thessaly who taught him.[13]

When Rhigas left school, presumably in his teens though the date is unknown, he became at first a schoolmaster himself. He taught at Kissos, another village on Mount Pelion a few miles south of Zagora. He must already have realised how dependent Greek schools were on text-books translated from foreign languages, especially French and German; and he aimed to master both languages himself. In particular, there was a dearth of elementary works on natural science in modern Greek, which he made it his business later to remedy. These experiences consolidated in his mind the conviction that education was the essential catalyst of liberation.

But was it sufficient for the purpose? It was only later experience that forced Rhigas to accept the necessity of armed rebellion as well. One of the reminiscences collected at Velestino in 1885, from an old man whose father had known Rhigas, was that he had later recruited by correspondence, as members of his revolutionary organisation, men from both Zagora and Kissos, presumably among his former school-fellows and pupils.[14] It is impossible to be sure that the story is not part of the legend which grew up about Rhigas after his death. But there is good evidence for the tradition that an incident in his teaching career was the first to bring home to him the inevitability of revolution. Local memories gave more than one version of what is basically the same story.[15]

4

One version was used in a poem dedicated to Rhigas by George Zalokostas (1805–58). The poem describes how he witnessed a humiliating scene outside a wayside church, while on his way back to Velestino from Kissos at Christmas, after a year as a schoolmaster. As the congregation came out of the church, armed Turks seized them for forced labour. Rhigas was himself compelled to carry a sack of grain, although he offered payment to escape the humiliation. He vowed vengeance on the oppressors, and began from that day to compose and sing his revolutionary songs.

In another version, related by a muleteer on Mount Pelion in 1885, the humiliating incident occurred when Rhigas was returning home from Constantinople to visit his family; in other words, at a later date, after he had emigrated from Thessaly. An armed Turk compelled Rhigas to carry him across a river in spate near Velestino. But in mid-stream Rhigas flung the Turk into the river and drowned him—a story which gives the earliest example of his legendary strength. He then ran to his home, embraced his mother, and told her what had happened. He took a loaf of bread and hurried to Volos, to take ship back to Constantinople. In this version, as in the first, his father does not figure at all.

A third, more circumstantial version, which was current among the villagers of Velestino, seems more convincing.[16] The story takes place one January, when Rhigas was 25 years old. (His age can only be approximate: it would imply that the year was 1782, but in fact he must have left home some years earlier.) He had returned, it was said, from Kissos to Velestino, and was accompanying his father on a visit to relatives in a neighbouring village. At this village they met a Turk from Velestino called Mustapha Suleiman, who was bitterly hostile to Rhigas's father. He demanded peremptorily from the father a quantity of *raki* (alcoholic spirit) and three gold pieces, threatening to run him through with a sword if he did not instantly obey. Rhigas angrily challenged him to do his worst. The Turk drew his sword, but other villagers intervened and succeeded in calming both parties.

The next morning Rhigas and his father set out to return to Velestino. Mustapha Suleiman overtook them on horseback, accompanied by five other Turks (or even Christians, according to variant sources). The Turk dismounted and compelled Rhigas

5

to carry some of the load from his horse; he also compelled the father to carry him for some distance, till they reached a spring whose classical name was Hypereia (in modern Greek, Kephalovrysi). There the incident ended, but Mustapha Suleiman continued to be vindictive towards Rhigas's father and his family.

Some time passed without a further clash, thanks to the Turkish *mudir* (governor) of Velestino, who was a friend of Rhigas's father, called Ahmed Ali. But he was later transferred and replaced, so Mustapha Suleiman decided to try again. Pretending to be friendly to Kyritzis, he invited him as a guest to a local Muslim festival, making it clear that he would regard a refusal as an act of hostility. Unaware that there was a plot to kill him, Rhigas's father accepted. On his way to the celebration, he met a group of Turks who were in league with Mustapha Suleiman. One of them, who was carrying a carcass of meat, said he was tired and asked the others to take it over. Rhigas's father volunteered to do so himself.

As they went on their way, they were met by a Turk who worked in Kyritzis's factory. Suspecting a plot against his employer, this Turk signalled to him to make his escape. Kyritzis accordingly dropped his load and ran. Mustapha Suleiman's party pursued him and fired at him, but he escaped. After running all day, he arrived at the village of Kerameidi, on the southern point of Mount Pelion. When Rhigas heard of what had happened to his father, he decided to leave Velestino for ever, and to move elsewhere, 'wherever fate might take him'. The whole episode naturally hardened his attitude towards the Turks, and fired his ambition for freedom.

He went to join his father at Kerameidi for a week; then they parted for good. He told his father to return home, to guard his family, to flatter the Turks, and to live through the bad times as best he could. After receiving his father's blessing, he took ship for Mount Athos, where he spent some time among the monasteries. Then he returned clandestinely, not to Mount Pelion but to the village of Litochorion on Mount Olympus, where his relative (a cousin or uncle) Spyro Ziras was serving as an *armatolos*. The *armatoloi* were nominally gendarmes in the service of the Turks against the *klephtes* or bandits, but as often as not the *armatoloi* and the klephtes were indistinguishable in practice. For a short time Rhigas served in Ziras's band, but he was still determined to escape abroad.

When he learned of Rhigas's intention, Ziras urged him not to leave the country; but if he must, then first to return to Mount Athos and consult Kosmas, the Abbot of Vatopedi. On their last night at Litochorion, the two drank a toast together, and in a wave of patriotic emotion Rhigas is said to have sung for the first time the famous lines:

Better one hour of life in freedom
Than forty years of bondage and prison!

Later this couplet was to form part of his *Thourios*, or War Hymn; but years passed before the poem took its final form.

The date of Rhigas's departure from home is uncertain. A common assumption is that it was in 1774, because Christopher Perrhaivos, the only biographer who knew him personally, says that he was then 17 years of age. Perrhaivos is unreliable about dates, especially in his *Short Biography*, which was published in 1860 when he was a very old man. But the age of 17 is given in the preface to his much earlier work, *War Memoirs*, published in 1836.[17] Even so, Perrhaivos only knew Rhigas from 1793, so the date is not unchallengeable. An ingeniously subjective argument has also been advanced that Rhigas was only 16 at the date of his departure.[18]

Perrhaivos complicates the question by saying in the *Short Biography* that Rhigas was only 35 when he was executed in 1797.[19] That is doubly inaccurate, since in fact he was executed in 1798 at the age of 40 (or perhaps 41). Perrhaivos's statement would mean that he was born in 1762, and could not possibly have left home for good, after the adventures described, in 1774. It would then have to be supposed that he left home in 1779, when he would have been 22–23 rather than 17. This is a perfectly possible date, if Perrhaivos's inaccuracies are allowed to cancel each other out. The case for a date several years later than 1774 has been independently argued, partly on the ground that Rhigas was then too young to have started his career at Constantinople and partly because in 1774 the Near East was in a state of turmoil.[20] But on the other hand, the state of unrest in the East may have been the actual reason for his leaving home.

Russia and Turkey had been at war since 1768. The Russian Empress, Catherine the Great, had deliberately spread the war into the Aegean in 1770 by sending the Orlov brothers to provoke a Greek rising. The rebellion was brutally crushed by the Sultan, Abdul Hamid, who then ordered the extermination of the Greek population. Although terrible destruction was carried out by Albanian troops sent into Greece for the purpose, the worst of the consequences were averted through the intervention of two influential Greeks, both of whom later played a part in Rhigas's own career.

Alexander Ypsilantis (1726–1806), who was then briefly Dragoman of the Porte (Secretary of State), secured the reversal of the Sultan's decree in 1774 before relinquishing his post. Nicholas Mavroyenis (1738–90), who was secretary to the *Kapudan Pasha* (the Commander-in-Chief of the Navy), helped in pacifying the Peloponnese, which was an important step in his own career. The Russo-Turkish war ended later in 1774 with the Treaty of Küchük Kainardji, which gave the Greeks a certain degree of protection under Russian auspices.

These events only affected Rhigas's life insofar as they exacerbated the perennial bitterness between Greeks and Turks. How long after them he left Thessaly can only be a matter of conjecture. It is impossible to estimate how long he spent moving between Thessaly, Mount Athos, Litochorion, Mount Athos again, and finally Constantinople. A date between 1777 and 1780 seems more plausible than 1774. It allows more time for his teaching career in Thessaly, and less time to be filled with guesswork on his arrival in Constantinople.

Whichever the date, Rhigas was then launched on his great but precarious adventure. His father returned to Velestino when Mustapha Suleiman died, apparently not long after Rhigas's departure. Rhigas wrote to his father from Constantinople urging him to arrange a suitable marriage for his sister Asimo, since he would not return himself 'before achieving his purpose'. Accordingly Kyritzis gave his daughter in matrimony to Antonios Kostoglou, a 'poor but cultivated' young man at Velestino.[21]

All of them were destined to a tragic end. Kyritzis was shot dead by a son of Mustapha Suleiman. When news of Rhigas's

8

rebellious activities reached the Turks at Velestino, presumably in 1798, they broke into the family home, hanged Asimo and impaled her husband. Their only son, who lived further south at Domokos, was tracked down and murdered by Turks from Velestino. Only Rhigas's mother and his brother Kostis survived the massacre, having already emigrated themselves to join him abroad.

The cruelty described by tradition seems almost unbelievable, and some of it may owe more to hostile legend than to historical fact. But the bitterness between Turkish masters and Greek rebels in the late eighteenth century is a fact which defies exaggeration. There were cases of peaceful coexistence, of which examples were the good relations that Rhigas's father had with his Turkish workmen, and even with the Turkish mayor of Velestino. At the same time, the capacity for irrational brutality was never far below the surface on either side. Rhigas witnessed and experienced it himself. He wrote years later, in a footnote to his translation from the Abbé Barthélemy's *Voyage of the young Anacharsis*, that 'many illegal killings of Christians' took place at Velestino.[22] The time was to come when these would be reciprocated. But a major part of his own life's work was to try, vainly as it turned out, to end the cycle of racial and religious enmity. He blamed it not on the Greek and Turkish peoples, but on the vicious corruption of Ottoman rule, tyrannising over both alike.

What then was to be his course of action? The first step was to enlarge his own education; and next, that of his fellow-countrymen. At what stage Rhigas concluded that revolutionary action was morally imperative can only be conjectured, since there are no certain dates in his early career. In 1776, when he was perhaps somewhere between Thessaly and Constantinople, a revolution had in fact broken out in a faraway country about which most people in south-east Europe knew nothing. There is no evidence that the American War of Independence made any impact whatever on Rhigas's imagination. No mention of America or Britain is to be found in anything that he wrote. Like all Greeks of his time, Rhigas was first and foremost a European. It was to Europe—Russia, Austria, Germany or France—that he looked for his country's salvation. But England, let alone America, was beyond his horizon.

[1] Legrand, 58–9.
[2] Amantos (1930), 122–3.
[3] Amantos (1948), 669.
[4] Vranousis (1953), 266, n. 1.
[5] Enepekidis (1965), 25; Amantos (1930), viii, n. 1.
[6] Pouqueville, III, 175.
[7] N. G. Politis, 13–16.
[8] Finlay, V. 281, n. 2.
[9] Oikonomidis, 135.
[10] Nikarousis (1929), 10.
[11] Vranousis (1953), 399.
[12] Perrhaivos (1860), 30–1.
[13] Ibid., 2–3.
[14] N. G. Politis, 14.
[15] *Ibid.*, 14–15.
[16] *Ibid.*, 15.
[17] Perrhaivos (1836), 16, fn.
[18] Pistas (1971), 5.
[19] Perrhaivos (1860), 40.
[20] Mikhalopoulos (1948), 403–4; Vranousis (1953), 11.
[21] N. G. Politis, 16.
[22] Rhigas, *Anacharsis*, IV (1797), 133; Vranousis (1953), 342, n. 7.

I I

APPRENTICESHIP TO CONFLICT

ALTHOUGH the story of Rhigas's youth contains much that is legendary, it also reveals much of the society in which he grew up. The oppressiveness of Ottoman misrule was arbitrary but intermittent. So far as the Greek villages were concerned, the administration varied from indifferent to non-existent. The Orthodox Church was expected to guarantee the good behaviour of the Greeks; if that did not work, it depended on the *armatoloi*; and if they failed, as they often did, the Turkish forces took matters into their own hands with crude brutality. Law and order were therefore precarious. To maintain them was officially the function of local governors (*pashas*), but some of them were regularly in a state of rebellion against their Sultan. In Rhigas's lifetime the most notorious of them were Osman Pasvanoglou, Pasha of Vidin in modern Bulgaria, and Ali Pasha of Epiros, neither of whom was in fact a Turk. The security of the Greeks and other peoples of south-east Europe depended on the whims of such men as these and their subordinate officials. A Christian had to pay a poll-tax (*kharaj*) simply in return for the right to keep his head on his shoulders. Only a Turk was allowed to carry arms or to ride a horse. The Turks could humiliate the Greeks with forced labour. But they in turn were humiliated by the quickwittedness of the Greeks.

In rural Greece there were few Turkish schoolmasters or merchants; even in the cities they were outnumbered by their Greek equivalents. An impoverished Turk would be ready to work alongside Greeks in a workshop managed by a Greek; Turkish girls were to be found as domestic servants in Greek households. On a personal level, there could even be friendly relations between Greeks and Turks, as the story of Rhigas's father showed, and as Rhigas's own experience was to confirm.

To an intelligent young Greek, the social system was at best unnatural, at worst intolerable. As a few months' service in a band of *armatoloi* must have convinced him, although movements of rebellion were inevitable and necessary, they could not by themselves restore Greek independence. Nor could education by itself. They needed to be complemented by other assets at a higher level of social activity: political influence, money, propaganda, and perhaps foreign help. Moreover, these things were needed just as much by the Muslim subjects of the Ottoman Empire as by the Christians.

When he arrived in the capital, Rhigas found a new kind of obstacle to the redemption of his people. Here there was a class of Greeks to whom the idea of independence had limited appeal, because they were already situated at the centre of Ottoman power. This community included three main groups, in ascending order of importance: the merchants, who knew that any rebellion against Ottoman rule could be fatal to their own interests; the Partriarchate and its senior clergy, who had formed virtually a branch of the Ottoman administration ever since the fall of Constantinople in 1453; and most powerful of all, the Phanariote aristocracy, whose palatial homes were concentrated in the district of the lighthouse (*phanari*). To their credit, in all three groups there were exceptional patriots who were prepared to risk their lives and livelihood in the cause of freedom. But naturally a young Greek on his first arrival in the capital could not tell which they were. So Rhigas adopted the sensible policy of seeking to penetrate the two groups which were penetrable. Not being a priest, he could not penetrate the Patriarchate; but he could become a merchant, and he could obtain employment among the Phanariotes. Within a few years he had done both.[1] He also set about widening his education.

In his early years at Constantinople, he is said to have devoted himself 'to commerce and to study'.[2] But he also soon found his way into the family circle of one of the most powerful Phanariotes, Alexander Ypsilantis. There is a tantalising absence of clues to the steps in Rhigas's progress at this stage, but a possibility is suggested by the story that when he visited the Monastery of Vatopedi on his way to Constantinople, the Abbot Kosmas gave him a letter of introduction to the Russian Ambassador.[3] The Ypsilantis family belonged to the pro-Russian wing of Phanariote politics; eventually they emigrated to Russia, where Alexander's three grandsons (Alexander, Dimitrios and Nicholas) played notable roles a generation later in organising the Greek revolution of 1821. It may have been Kosmas's introduction which indirectly brought Rhigas within the family circle.

Alexander Ypsilantis's career was typical of the strange system under which the Ottoman Empire was governed. He held a succession of the posts which were reserved for favoured families of the Greek aristocracy, including those of Dragoman of the Porte (meaning strictly Court Interpreter, but in fact a post of great influence) and Hospodar (Governor) successively of both the Danubian principalities, Vallachia and Moldavia. He was more than once obliged by circumstances to resign from office; his career underwent many other vicissitudes, but it was not until 1806 that he finally suffered the fate of so many ambitious Phanariotes, being beheaded at the age of 80.

At more than one stage, Rhigas's life was closely involved with the Ypsilantis family. To begin with, probably in the early 1780s, he was educated together with Alexander's two sons, Constantine and Dimitrios, who were a few years younger than himself.[4] These years of what may be called Rhigas's higher education were extremely valuable to him. He learned French, Italian and German thoroughly; he studied the Ottoman system of government at close quarters; and he formed personal contacts both with the Phanariotes and with the commercial community at a privileged level. In later years he had many commercial correspondents at Constantinople, even though he had been absent from the city for ten years.

Trade would have been beneath the dignity of his fellow-students, the Ypsilantis brothers. From them, and from their father, Rhigas learned that a Phanariote could also be a Greek patriot. His horizon was further widened in or about 1785, when Alexander Ypsilantis promoted him to be his private secretary. It is not easy to make out how long this appointment lasted, or how it ended. According to one version, Rhigas accompanied Ypsilantis to Yassy when he was appointed Hospodar of Moldavia in 1787; but after a quarrel between them, Rhigas left Yassy for Bucharest and entered the service of Nicholas Mavroyenis, who had been appointed Hospodar of Vallachia in 1786.[5] According to another source, Ypsilantis himself introduced Rhigas to Mavroyenis;[6] but this source mistakenly believed that Mavroyenis was Hospodar of Moldavia at the time.

According to Perrhaivos, Rhigas was introduced to Mavroyenis by a wealthy hellenised Romanian aristocrat called Brancoveanu, who was his first employer at Bucharest.[7] It is not clear to which member of the Brancoveanu family Perrhaivos refers. Most probably it was Emmanuel, the father of Gregorios Brancoveanu (1785–1854), who was to be a supporter of the Greek revolution in 1821. Romanian historians, however, have found no trace of Rhigas's employment by any member of the family.[8]

Phanariote intrigues are never easy to disentangle, but a more or less reasonable reconstruction can be made. Alexander Ypsilantis was hoping to achieve the liberation of Greece through the dissolution of the Ottoman Empire. He counted on the help of Catherine the Great of Russia and the Emperor Joseph II of Austria, who had formed an alliance with this end in view as early as 1780. Mavroyenis was a *novus homo* who had risen to power by his own talents, his father having been the Austrian Vice-Consul on Mykonos. Having made his name by pacifying the Peloponnese after the revolt prompted by the Orlov brothers, he had been promoted as Dragoman of the Fleet. In contrast with Ypsilantis, he favoured the *status quo* in the Ottoman Empire, and consequently supported the pro-French policy which the Sultan had adopted.[9]

It has therefore been surmised that, so far from quarrelling with Ypsilantis (an unlikely gesture for a rising young man), Rhigas was used by Ypsilantis to serve as a watchdog over Mavroyenis. On this hypothesis, Ypsilantis sent Rhigas to Bucharest in 1786 with an introduction to Brancoveanu, before the arrival of Mavroyenis as Hospodar. Brancoveanu employed him for a few months, until Mavroyenis arrived. Rhigas was then introduced to Mavroyenis, who was impressed by his abilities, and offered him employment. This accords reasonably well with Perrhaivos's account, which he must have heard from Rhigas.

Ypsilantis's plans were upset in 1787, however, when war broke out again between Russia and Turkey. The war of 1787–92 gave Mavroyenis the opportunity to rise to still greater eminence, though eventually it brought about his undoing. For Ypsilantis, the war was an immediate disaster. His intrigues with the Sultan's enemies became known at the capital; he was forced to escape to Austria; and Yassy was occupied by the Russian army.

It is not clear to what extent Rhigas would have been a conscious party to his patron's plans. While he was in Ypsilantis's service, he would naturally have adopted his employer's point of view that Russia was the power to be trusted as the Greeks' potential liberator. At that stage of his life, before 1789, there was no reason to look to France to fulfil that role. In any case, there is no evidence yet that Rhigas had formed a mature political outlook. He was still, in the words of an early biographer, 'dividing his time between commercial affairs and his favourite studies'.[10]

If his sympathies began to shift towards the French while he was at Bucharest, the reasons were not political, nor was the shift due to Mavroyenis's pro-French attitude. Rhigas had little reason to enjoy the company of his new employer. Although not a Phanariote, Mavroyenis had all the unattractive characteristics of the ruling class. A Romanian historian gives a sketch of his character: quick-tempered, violent, brutal, cruel and inhumane.[11] He used his position to acquire a vast fortune. Rhigas's own opinion of him is recorded in the manuscript of one of his earliest works, where a footnote, deleted but still visible, describes Mavroyenis as 'an abortion of human nature, and worthless as Hospodar of Vallachia'.[12] His nephew (or cousin) Ioannis played an equally disagreeable role in a later phase of Rhigas's biography.

What turned Rhigas's sympathies in a new direction was the cultural environment in which he found himself. Bucharest was a city where his talents were bound to flourish. It was the most sophisticated capital of the Balkans, rivalled only by the sister-capital of Yassy. It had close contacts with Europe; its educational facilities were highly developed; the commercial community was large and prosperous. Although Vallachia and Moldavia were nominally under Ottoman rule, in both capitals of the Danubian principalities a Greek was instinctively at home; Turks were actually forbidden to settle there; Romanians, though already becoming nationally conscious, still accepted Greek as the language of cultivated society. Rhigas's role as secretary to Brancoveanu and Mavroyenis was much more than a clerical one: he conducted their political correspondence and held considerable responsibility. He was known as the *Grammatikos*; but the word means not only a clerk but a man of letters.[13]

Contemporary sketch of Rhigas by Nicholas Moskhovakis
(National Historical Museum, Athens).

Rhigas's surviving portraits, some of which belong to this period, show a striking if not a handsome figure. His appearance and character were described by Perrhaivos a few years later, but in so short a life a few years would make little difference:

> He was of average height, with a thick neck, a round red-and-white face, a mouth of average width, fair moustache, rather broad nose, light blue eyes, bushy eyebrows, wide forehead, bulky temples, large ears, darkish hair, and a decidedly large, round, powerful head. Psychologically, his merits were charm and intelligence; a lively nature, articulate, industrious, of simple habits, sympathetic; the persuasiveness on his lips attracted everyone to his advice; he had no respect for a Greek's ancestry, but only for his conduct; he often, indeed, rebuked those who took pride in their family or city when they were themselves of bad character.[14]

The portraits bear out Perrhaivos's description, though some of them do not conceal a certain flabbiness, while seeking to emphasise heroic qualities. The summary of his character readily accounts for his dislike of Mavroyenis and the Phanariotes.

Some allowance must be made for the fact that Perrhaivos was a devoted admirer, who knew Rhigas only in the last five years of his life. There were other views of his character held by those who knew him in less dramatic circumstances. The most bitter of his critics was Michael Perdikaris, who was a medical student at Bucharest and spent some time in his company while Rhigas was still secretary to Brancoveanu. In later life, Perdikaris was an unsuccessful writer, whose attacks on others were wild and often inconsistent. He regarded the betrayal of Rhigas in 1797 as 'the salvation of the whole Greek race', and described him as 'vicious and dissolute, inclined to sensuality and absolutely full of corruption of every kind, as all would agree who happened to have the slightest knowledge of the man'. But he also admitted that Rhigas was energetic, quick-witted, persuasive, eloquent, and 'not without a smattering of education'. Moreover, he castigated as well as defended the man who betrayed Rhigas to the Austrian police.[15]

Most of Rhigas's friends remembered him differently. They were of several nationalities at Bucharest: French, Austrian, Romanian, even Turkish as well as Greek. They embraced many classes of society: scholars and teachers, merchants, officials and diplomats, writers and artists. In the French community a particular friend was Alexandre, Comte d'Hauterive (1754–1830), an *attaché* to the French Embassy at Constantinople, who had served as political secretary to the Hospodar of Moldavia before being transferred to Bucharest. This friendship might have played a part in securing Rhigas's later appointment as interpreter at the French Consulate in Bucharest (though it has been a matter of dispute whether he in fact held such a post). At any rate, since d'Hauterive was a member of the pre-revolutionary aristocracy who survived to have a distinguished career in diplomacy and politics, his friendship must have helped to widen Rhigas's European horizon.

Among his Romanian friends were Iordache (George) Slătineanu, a Hellenist and member of the Greco-Dacian Literary Society, who translated works of Metastasio into both Greek and

Romanian; and Iordache Golescu, a lexicographer of the Romanian language and an enthusiastic cartographer, like Rhigas himself. In 1797, when Rhigas published his maps of Greece and the Danubian principalities, Golescu honoured him with an epigram in Greek; so did a Greek friend at Vienna, Stephen Kommitas, who was later to become head of the Bucharest Academy.[16] Whether at Bucharest or Vienna, Rhigas remained in correspondence with such friends, as his address-book showed after his arrest.[17]

Romanians and Greeks were naturally his closest associates. They shared a patriotic yearning to be free, even if their prison was, comparatively speaking, a gilded cage. Rhigas might easily have been content with his civilised life. Success in business made him a wealthy merchant, as he was later described.[18] The influence of his official employers gave him access to the Academy, first as a student and probably later as a teacher.[19] His cultural interests ranged wide: literature and the natural sciences, history and geography, the classics and foreign languages, music and poetry. A favourite pastime was to accompany popular songs on the flute. He was at ease in any company.

It is not easy to list with certainty all his circle of friends, nor to be sure when he first knew them, because many of them moved to and fro, as he did himself, between Bucharest, Yassy and Vienna. His name was sometimes linked with contemporaries as a matter of supposition, without positive evidence: for example, with his employer's relative, Ioannis Mavroyenis, whom he certainly knew later at Vienna, or with Constantine Stamatis, who later became a French agent in the Danubian principalities.[20] But their later contacts do not prove earlier acquaintance at Bucharest. It is also not easy to distinguish the acquaintances of his first period there (1786–90) and his second (1791–96). A reasonable conjecture is that in the first period his connections were primarily cultural and intellectual; in the second, commercial and political. A few names stand out, in the early period, from the closely-knit community of Greeks. Among them were Daniel Philippidis and Grigorios Konstantas, who collaborated in publishing a *New Geography*, of which Rhigas had a copy in his baggage when it was seized by the Austrian police in December 1797. Another was Lambros Photiadis, a poet and scholar who was, like Rhigas, close to the Brancoveanu family, and later became head of the Bucharest Academy. Others give personal glimpses of Rhigas which are valuable because so rare at this stage of his life: Nicholas Moskhovakis, who made two drawings of him which survive; and the poet Alexander Kalphoglou, who wrote a jocular epigram on the sight of Rhigas rolling a barrel through the snow.[21] Of the older generation, the most influential of those whom Rhigas came to know at the Academy were two outstanding teachers: Joseph Moisiodakas and Dimitrios Katartzis (the latter also called Photiadis).

Moisiodakas, born about 1730, was a pioneer of educational reform at Yassy and Bucharest. He taught the classics, mathematics, the natural sciences, and specifically geography. He was criticised by academic colleagues for his unconventional attitude to the teaching of the Greek language, especially the classics. Although he admired the ancient writers, he thought it absurd to treat antiquity as a golden age of virtue and justice; at the same time he pointed to 'the scarcity, or rather the total absence, of most of the works of antiquity'. In an epigrammatic summary of his views, he declared that 'today, Greece suffers from two faults—respect for, and indifference to, antiquity'.[22] Above all, he abhorred the pedantic teaching of grammar, and he urged the use of demotic Greek for all purposes. These iconoclastic theories led to his persecution by most contemporary pedagogues, but earned for him the warm respect of Rhigas. It must have been gratifying to the old man that during his life-time, in 1796–97, Rhigas included a specific identification of his birthplace, at Cernovadă on the lower Danube, in his great *Map of Hellas*.

Katartzis, who was approaching 70 years of age, had a similar and perhaps even stronger influence on Rhigas.[23] Apart from teaching at the Academy, he held high office under the Hospodars at Bucharest, first as president of the Supreme Court and later as Grand Chancellor. From him Rhigas learned Arabic and Turkish, which extended his interests eastwards beyond the Balkans just as his knowledge of French and German extended them westwards. Like Moisiodakas, Katartzis also impressed on him the importance of using the demotic language for all purposes—literary, scientific and administrative. In the debate on the language question which absorbed the intellecutals of the Danubian principalities in the late eighteenth century, it seems that Katartzis, unlike Moisiodakas, avoided making personal enemies. He was attacked only by Michael Perdikaris, an unsurprising exception.

While he was enlarging his education and his view of the world in the late 1780s, soon after his thirtieth birthday, Rhigas was already engaged on his own first writings. Among them, no doubt under the influence of Moisiodakas, was said to be a 'scheme for the education of young Greeks', which is not extant.[24] The earliest surviving examples from his pen were a scientific text-book for students and a collection of adaptations of French novelettes, both written in the 'simple Greek' or demotic language. But with a Greek's aptitude for diversity, he was simultaneously engaged in much other business as well.

He was now an established businessman. By 1788 he was the owner of a property in the district of Vlasca, south-west of Bucharest. There he was able to install his mother and his younger brother, Kostis. A few years later he was active in public duties on behalf of the neighbourhood where he resided in Bucharest.[25] Apart from his growing prosperity, his status in the service of the Hospodar also gave him a social prominence and a political role.

The most important episode in his public career came during the Russo-Turkish war of 1787–92, in which Austria also took part on the side of Russia from 1788. When the allies invaded the principalities, Nicholas Mavroyenis at first inspired a successful resistance to the Austrian attack on Vallachia. In Moldavia, on the other hand, the resistance to the Russians was feeble, and Alexander Ypsilantis had deserted his post. As a result, Mavroyenis was appointed Commander-in-Chief of the Sultan's forces in both principalities.[26] His qualifications for high command, however, were administrative rather than strategic. He had almost no experience of warfare against a major military power.

There were also suspicions of disloyalty against him, not only because he was a Greek. As the son of an Austrian Vice-Consul, he had been brought up in an Austrophile environment. Among his subordinates was an expatriate Austrian, probably of Greek descent, called Christodoulos Theodorou Kirlian, who was a local governor in Vallachia. Mavroyenis also had to make use of the persistently independent Pasha of Vidin, Osman Pasvanoglou, who had ambitions of his own to seize control of the Danubian principalities. A role of some importance, though not precisely defined, was played during the war by Rhigas himself, whose sympathies cannot have lain either with Mavroyenis or with the Sultan whom he was nominally serving.[27]

Kirlian played an equivocal role which served Austrian rather than Turkish interests; and he was rewarded by the Emperor after the war. As for the roles of Pasvanoglou and Rhigas, the principal source is Perrhaivos, who must have heard the story from Rhigas himself. Mavroyenis assigned an administrative post to Rhigas in the district of Craiova, in the south-west corner of Vallachia immediately north of the Danube. His function was to ensure an orderly transit of the river by the Turkish forces from the south. The crossing-place was at Vidin, on the south bank, controlled by Pasvanoglou.

Pasvanoglou's loyalties were always doubtful. He was by birth a Bosnian, said to be of Catholic descent. His father had been disgraced and executed by the Sultan of his day. Osman, the son, had formed an irregular force of many different nationalities, both Muslim and Christian, with which he fought his way back to pre-eminence in the vicinity of Vidin, where the Sultan formally appointed him as Pasha with much the same reluctance as he recognised Ali Pasha at Ioannina. Although Pasvanoglou had no love for the Sultan, he made his independent force of some 1200 men available to support the Turkish Army in 1788–89.

In the winter of 1789–90, Pasvanoglou's force crossed the Danube from Vidin to Craiova, where Rhigas was installed. Severe conditions made it difficult to supply the force's needs. In charge of the commissariat was a man who happened, unknown to Pasvanoglou, to be the uncle of Mavroyenis. Pasvanoglou accused him of incompetence, and struck him in the course of their quarrel. The offended official complained to the Hospodar, who ordered Pasvanoglou's arrest. Pasvanoglou tried to escape in disguise back to Vidin. Then Rhigas, who had received Mavroyenis's order that Pasvanoglou was to be taken dead or alive, intervened to save him. He sent four men who would be able to recognise the disguised Pasha to intercept his flight, and arranged a personal meeting in secret. He advised Pasvanoglou to retire to Vidin and lie low, leaving matters in his own hands.[28]

Meanwhile the Russian army had overrun Moldavia and was advancing on Bucharest. The Turkish forces retreated in confusion across the Danube, accompanied by Mavroyenis. Within a few days, according to Perrhaivos, Mavroyenis himself was disgraced and executed. Ostensibly his execution was an act of revenge by a newly appointed Turkish Vizier, whose brother had earlier been executed by Mavroyenis at Bucharest; but in reality the reasons were probably the suspicion of treachery and the total failure of his command. Perrhaivos adds that Rhigas himself was a witness of Mavroyenis's execution.[29]

Some of the details of this story are implausible. It is difficult to believe that Pasvanoglou was really in danger from the demoralised force under Mavroyenis's command, when he had his own 1200 irregulars as a body-guard. It is also impossible that Rhigas could have witnessed Mavroyenis's execution, which took place at the beginning of October 1790, when Rhigas is known to have been in Vienna. The motives of the various participants in the story bear the stamp of legend, if not of fantasy. But there is undoubtedly circumstantial evidence that Rhigas performed some valuable service for Pasvanoglou, for which he was deeply grateful.

Rhigas returned to Bucharest, which was then under Russian occupation, in the spring of 1790. Since the downfall of Mavroyenis left him without official employment, he accepted the post of secretary to Kirlian, who was leaving in June for Vienna. There he hoped to be able to publish some of his literary works, on which he had already been engaged. Before their departure from Bucharest, Pasvanoglou arrived to thank Rhigas for his services.

Perrhaivos records Rhigas's own account of their meeting. Speaking in Turkish, Rhigas gave Pasvanoglou a lecture on the duties of men to each other. No one, he said, has a right to oppress his fellow-men, who are all children of God, on grounds of religion. The words are those of Perrhaivos, over seventy years after the event, but the thoughts are those of Rhigas:

We have neither seen nor heard nor found it written in any book that God punished one man because he was a Turk nor another because he was a Christian, nor another because he was a worshipper of the sun and the moon, etc. We see, however, and we hear and we find it written in books that God punished, and always punishes, those who tyrannise over His creation, their brothers.[30]

Pasvanoglou promised, says Perrhaivos, that he would follow Rhigas's advice as if it were from his father.

Rhigas felt encouraged to go further. He urged Pasvanoglou to crush those of his subordinate beys and agas who oppressed the people of Vidin and elsewhere, and 'to embrace the good Turks and their unhappy subjects'. He warned the Pasha that the Sultan would react with hostility to such a deviation from what he would call 'the way of God and the decrees of the Koran'. But he proposed, somewhat naively, that when the Sultan wrote disapprovingly to him, Pasvanoglou should forward his letters to Rhigas, who would advise him how to reply. God would also be on his side, and he should remember that evil-doers were always cowards who feared the wrath of God. There were, he concluded, many examples to prove this, both in the past and particularly 'in the present events in France'.[31] If Perrhaivos was not simply exercising his imagination, this was Rhigas's first reported reference to the French Revolution.

Pasvanoglou promised to follow his advice, though there is no evidence that he ever did so. Subsequently he revolted more than once against the Sultan, but he showed a remarkable capacity for survival, and died a natural death in 1807. The two are said to have become 'blood-brothers' (*adelphopoitoi*) as a result of this episode.[32] How seriously Pasvanoglou took this relationship can only be conjectured. But in Rhigas's case not only Perrhaivos's biography but also his own writings testify that his sympathy with the Turks, as fellow-victims of Ottoman tyranny with the Greeks, was wholly sincere.

His attitude is further illustrated by the story that he formed a private society of friends (*hetairia*), encouraged by Alexander Ypsilantis, to which Turks as well as Greeks were admitted.[33] At one time historians believed that it was a branch of a Masonic Lodge called the *Society of Good Cousins*; but this is impossible, because the *Good Cousins* was an alternative name of the Italian

Carbonari, who were not even established in Rhigas's life-time.[34] There is no positive evidence to connect Rhigas with Freemasonry at any date. Only one of his close associates was ever alleged to be a Mason, and that was after Rhigas's death.[35] On the other hand, his Greco-Turkish society is supported by at least one well-informed source.

Nicholas Ypsilantis, a son of Constantine and grandson of Alexander, was one of the organisers of the later *Philiki Hetairia* which launched the revolution of 1821. He wrote the following account in his memoirs:

> Using as magnet a fraternity which he had established, Rhigas succeeded gradually in drawing forth his compatriots from the depths of the forests and the caves in the rocks which they used as refuges, and uniting them under a single oath with the Muslim rebels. He swore them on the Gospel to support each other unto death and to call each other by the name of 'blood-brothers' [*adelphopoitoi*], signifying the close link which they had between them. From that day to this, we see with great astonishment Greeks sacrifice their life for Turks who are their brothers, protecting them in misfortune, providing them with the means to return freely to their homes, and even themselves escorting them for greater security. The Turks behaved similarly to the Greeks who were their brothers . . .
>
> With this celebrated society (*hetairia*) Rhigas succeeded in a short time in softening the sufferings of his compatriots, and on this he based half his hopes . . . However, these prerequisites ceased to exist later, and when the leaders of the new *hetairia* set about continuing the work of Rhigas's fraternity, they ceased to accept Turks and limited themselves to Greek combatants alone.[36]

This is an idealised account of what Rhigas actually achieved. It owes much to the aspirations which he put on paper at a later date, and which Nicholas Ypsilantis certainly had read, such as the *Thourios* and the *New Political Order*. There is no reason to doubt, however, that Rhigas did try to create such a *hetairia*. Equally beyond doubt, it cannot have been a revolutionary body. If it had been such, it could not have included Turkish members, just as the later *Philiki Hetairia* could not. Whether or not Rhigas later formed a truly revolutionary *hetairia* is a much-disputed question; but if he did, it must have been distinct from the nonsectarian fraternity of 'blood-brothers' which Nicholas Ypsilantis describes.

Such intimate links between Greeks and Turks were rare, but Rhigas's initiative was not unprecedented. There were, for example, merchants' guilds (*esnaf*) among both Muslims and Christians in the Ottoman Empire, with some degree of inter-penetration between them.[37] In the organisation of such guilds, the senior members formed what was called a 'lodge' (*lonja* in Turkish; *lontza* in Greek). As a merchant himself, Rhigas might probably have belonged to such a guild, or set up a Greco-Turkish club on a similar model. The use of the term 'lodge' also suggests a possible explanation of the false connection with Freemasonry.

There is indirect evidence of Rhigas's good-will towards the Turks in the surviving accounts of his personal seal, which was intended to become the national seal of an independent Hellenic Republic. The seal itself was thrown into the sea at the time of his arrest at Trieste in December 1797. But details of it were recalled by two men who had seen it, Christopher Perrhaivos and George Kalaphatis. Although there are differences in their recollections of it, a more or less convincing reconstruction can be made of its design.

Perrhaivos described the seal as bearing three clubs inclined at an angle, with three crosses above them, and the inscription: 'For the Faith, for the Fatherland, the Laws and Freedom'.[38] Kalaphatis described it as bearing a single club (of Herakles), with three stars above, a half-moon below, and the inscription: 'Hellenic Republic, Freedom, Equality'.[39] Neither man's memory is likely to have been perfect, but Kalaphatis was speaking much nearer to the date when the seal was last to be seen. If it is assumed that Kalaphatis's three stars are the same as Perrhaivos's three crosses, then his half-moon could have been the Islamic crescent. Given also the omission by Kalaphatis of 'the Faith', by which Perrhaivos evidently meant Christianity, then Kalaphatis's description has a more ecumenical character and one more typical of Rhigas.

The conflicting stories reflect a confusion from which Rhigas was trying to free both himself and his fellow-countrymen. It was assumed by almost all Greeks that it was impossible to be a patriot (in Rhigas's vocabulary, a 'philhellene') without being anti-Turkish. Rhigas maintained that all men were brothers, and none superior to others. It was easier, not harder, for him to think of a Turk as his brother because he believed in the brotherhood of all Greeks. He would rebuke a Greek from Epiros for claiming to be more Greek than one from Thrace, pointing out ironically that the earliest known Greeks came, like himself, from Thessaly. What mattered was that in their own day, they were united by Christianity and patriotism. Arguments based on remote ancestry were irrelevant, and for that reason he was opposed to a premature revival of classical Greek until it could be studied for its own sake in freedom.[40]

Rhigas was deeply sensitive to the dynamic of national tradition, both historical and religious, in contributing to the emancipation of a people. He differed from most of his contemporaries in recognising and accepting that this applied to Muslims as well as Christians. Of the Greeks, he told Perrhaivos:

> From our ancestors before Christ we should acquire wisdom and morality and courage, which made them also immortal, and they left to us, their descendants, the indelible memory of freedom; but from our wise and saintly Fathers after Christ let us embrace their inspired commands, living as inseparable brothers through holy baptism.[41]

These words could only apply to the Greeks; but he also saw the Turks as brothers, and put the question to Pasvanoglou:

> When a father, for example, begets many sons, one of whom becomes a dervish and another a bektash, another a pasha, another an ulema, another a businessman, another a baker, and others take up other trades, can they deny their father and their brotherhood because of the difference of their occupations? Are men justified then before God in rejecting and condemning each other, when their Father loves all equally?[42]

Such was the underlying principle of 'blood-brotherhood'. Perrhaivos can be regarded as reliable in recalling the spirit, if not the letter, of Rhigas's words some sixty years after his death. He had himself heard what Rhigas said to his Greek friends, and he had heard Rhigas repeat what he said to Pasvanoglou. It is surprising only that his account of what Rhigas said is in each case closer in spirit to Kalaphatis's account of Rhigas's seal than to his own. The truth will never be known, but the more ecumenical depiction of the seal is the more probable, if only because it is the less obvious. Rhigas was not always an easy man for even his close friends to understand.

He was in a restless, undecided frame of mind in the aftermath of the war. Disappointments crowded upon him, although his own conduct had been irreproachable, and even successful within its limits. Bucharest was under enemy occupation; his official appointment was at an end; his previous employer, Mavroyenis, was dead in tragic circumstances. There was nothing to detain him in the Danubian principalities, and much to attract him abroad. The news from France in 1789 was stirring, but not easy to interpret from the remoteness of eastern Europe. The offer of continuing employment by Kirlian, whom he followed to Vienna in June 1790, opened up the prospect of a wider world. It also provided Rhigas with the opportunity of finding a publisher for works on which he had been engaged before the war. When he left Bucharest, as he wrote after his return, his baggage consisted of 'a pillow stuffed with my clothes and two manuscripts which I had to get printed at Vienna'.[43] Both were to be on the market before the end of the year.

❂ ❂ ❂

[1] Mikhalopoulos (1948), 404.
[2] Nicolopoulos, 1–2.
[3] N. G. Politis, 15.
[4] Philemon (1859), II. 10.
[5] MEE, s.v. Rhigas.
[6] Philemon (1859), II. 10–11.
[7] Perrhaivos (1860), 5.
[8] Oikonomidis, 132.
[9] Mikhalopoulos (1948), 406–8.
[10] Nicolopoulos, 1–2.
[11] Xénopol, II. 245–6.
[12] Vranousis (1953), 24–5.
[13] Pantelić, 43 ff.; Oikonomidis, 130 ff.
[14] Perrhaivos (1860), 30. On the por-

traits, see Lambros (1905), 631–40.
[15] Amantos (1948), 400.
[16] Camariano-Cioran (1974), 250; 346; 518.
[17] Legrand, 72–3.
[18] Pantazopoulos, 11, n. 20.
[19] Camariano-Cioran (1974), 447–9.
[20] MEE, s.v. I. Mavroyenis; K. Stamatis.
[21] Dimaras (1974), 163.
[22] Ibid., 146.
[23] Perrhaivos (1860) spells his name Kantartzis. Dimaras (1972), 148, gives his alternative name as Photiadis.
[24] Kordatos (1974), 87.

[25] Oikonomidis, 135–6; Vranousis (1953), 36–7.
[26] Nikarousis (1926), 569.
[27] Perrhaivos (1860), 5.
[28] *Ibid.*, 6–7.
[29] *Ibid.*, 8–9.
[30] *Ibid.*, 10.
[31] *Ibid.*, 11.
[32] Pantazopoulos, 12, n. 27.
[33] Philemon (1859), II. 13.
[34] Mavromikhalos, 123–4.

[35] Enepekidis (1955/b), 25–8.
[36] Kambouroglou, 101–2.
[37] R. J. Crampton, in Clogg (1981), 185–7.
[38] Perrhaivos (1860), 22–3 and fn.
[39] Theotokis, 39, n. 9.
[40] Perrhaivos (1860), 30.
[41] *Ibid.*, 32.
[42] *Ibid.*, 10.
[43] Laios (1955), 4.

III

THE CALL OF EUROPE

VIENNA in the middle of 1790 gave Rhigas his first experience of Europe outside the Ottoman Empire. It was exhilarating, but his experience with Kirlian was a bitter disappointment. Kirlian was a disagreeable and untrustworthy employer, though not valueless as a political patron. His background was obscure, but his first names—Christodoulos Theodorou—confirmed his Greek origin. Since he knew no western language, he had to rely on Rhigas even to translate an application to the Austrian Emperor for his ennoblement, in return for services in the recent war. The services were themselves dubious. His extravagant claim to have negotiated the Turkish withdrawal from Vallachia and the unimpeded entry of the Austrian army showed little loyalty to his nominal sovereign, the Sultan. But the Emperor must have been convinced, for on 16 August 1790 Kirlian was gazetted as Baron von Langenfeld.[1]

Langenfeld soon caused Rhigas acute embarrassment by withholding his salary and accusing him of embezzlement. For the time being, however, he valued the influence of his ambiguous patron. Rhigas had already some contacts in the Greek community of Austria, formed through earlier friendships in the Danubian principalities. Two known to have been close to him in 1790 and later were Dimitrakis Tournavitis, formerly a teacher at Bucharest, and Ioannis Mavroyenis, the nephew or cousin of the unfortunate Hospodar of Vallachia. But although the Greek community was large and cultivated, as well as predominant in trade with the Near East, it was not politically influential. To move in higher circles, Rhigas needed the influence of Langenfeld.

Some of his prominent contacts may have been formed only during his second visit to Vienna: for example, J. C. von Engel, the Hungarian historian, or Baron Gamerra, to whom Rhigas tried in vain to appeal for protection after his arrest in 1797. Others certainly belonged to his first visit: for example, the philhellene publisher Joseph von Baumeister, and even, if the story is true, the Chancellor Count von Kaunitz. Rhigas is said to have

The 'Griechen Beissel' tavern in Vienna where Greeks gathered during the time of Rhigas (archives of Dimitrios Karamberopoulos).

30

presented a plan to Kaunitz to promote a Greek rising by prolonging the war with Turkey.[2] The Greeks had already been encouraged to rise by Catherine of Russia, and a small armada was still operating from Trieste under the Greek privateer, Lambros Katsonis; but he was soon reduced to ineffectual piracy.

At least it appears that Rhigas was already pondering revolutionary plans. He saw that Greek liberation would not be achieved solely within the confines of Ottoman territory. A more ambitious conception of the struggle was needed. Independence required not only education, with which he had so far been concerned, but also power. Both needs pointed towards Europe. The Greeks needed foreign expertise to acquire a modern education, and support from abroad to strengthen their physical resources. For education, the natural sources to tap were French and German. For physical power and political pressure, the natural allies seemed at first to be Turkey's hostile neighbours, Russia and Austria; but the revolution of 1789 shifted the focus back to France. England was seen as the perennial enemy of France and the natural ally of Turkey; besides, English was a language which Rhigas never tried to master. America was too remote to be considered.

From 1790 onwards, Rhigas's mind seethed with activity of many kinds, not always well directed towards his goal. He had no doubt about France as a source of intellectual and political inspiration, so long as the Revolution of 1789 still seemed a benign and hopeful event. Germany was also a source of intellectual inspiration—it was remarkable how many of his Greek contemporaries were studying Kant—but Prussia was unlikely to exercise political power except in association with Austria. Austria and Russia were both great and potentially friendly powers, since both were still at war with Turkey in 1790; but either of them would have been more likely to present Greece with a new autocracy than with genuine liberty. Rhigas's mental vision embraced a kaleidoscope of possibilities in which all these nations played a part, but in 1790 only France had all the qualifications he sought.

He spent much of that year, both before and after his move from Bucharest to Vienna, in preparing for publication the first products of his pen. One was his collection of romantic novelettes called the *School of Delicate Lovers*; another was an educational text-book called the *Anthology of Physics*; both were published at Vienna in 1790.[3] There could hardly have been a sharper contrast between them, but that was implicit in the nature of his inspiration. He was trying to comprise the whole range of interests—and many more were to come—which education must have for his young compatriots. Lest the scale of the prospect might escape his readers, Rhigas added a note at the end of his *Anthology of Physics* stating that he was also engaged on a translation of Montesquieu's *Esprit des Lois*, so that no other Greek seeking to promote 'the benefit of the race' need undertake it.[4] But this work was never to reach publication.

The *School of Delicate Lovers* and the *Anthology of Physics* illustrate two aspects of Rhigas's conception of education, the moral and the scientific; but both were subordinated to his overriding conception of patriotism, which he called 'philhellenism'. This was a term which could not yet be applied to foreigners, as it was to be in 1821; there were too few of them to deserve the name. The Greeks alone, for the time being, must bear the whole burden of philhellenism.

The *School* (a term used in the same sense as a 'school of painters') contained adaptations of six stories by the French writer Rétif de la Bretonne. On the title-page they were called translations from the French, but the author was not named and was in fact never identified until more than a century and a half later.[5] The stories were extracted from the first four volumes, published in 1780, of a vast collection by Rétif under the title *Les Contemporaines, ou aventures des plus jolies femmes de l'âge présent*, which eventually ran to 42 volumes containing 261 stories.

The *Anthology* had a purely didactic purpose; at the same time, its 'philhellenic' motive was even more explicit. It was intended for 'intelligent Greeks who desire education', according to the preface, and was written in 'the simple style' so that all could understand it. The preface ended with the words: 'Let everyone contribute gladly what he will so that, with help on all sides, the fallen Greek race may be restored.'[6] By the standards of the day, this was virtually a revolutionary challenge.

The contents of the *Anthology of Physics* are a simple and straightforward summary of such scientific knowledge as was available at the time in French and German text-books. The most important single source, as has been established by Dr D. A.

Karamberopoulos, was the French *Encyclopédie*. The *Anthology* is written in the form of a dialogue between a pupil posing questions and a teacher answering them, so that almost the entire work is printed within inverted commas. There are 24 chapters, of which 18 are concerned with astronomy, meteorology and terrestrial science. The last six chapters deal with minerals, plants, lower forms of life, fish, birds and animals (including man). The work was evidently finished in haste, because notes are appended on other subjects which were not ready for formal treatment, such as magnetism, mercury and electricity.[7] It can be assumed for this reason that although published in the same year as the *School*, on which Rhigas had probably been working for much longer, the *Anthology* went to press later. Not for the last time among Rhigas's works, it has the defects of a hurried composition. But it gives a useful insight into his own methods of instruction.

The six stories in the *School of Delicate Lovers* show a more leisurely style of composition. They were compiled, he writes in the preface, 'to give a slight idea of the entertaining literature of Europe, which produces both amusement and a kind of moral improvement'; at the same time, he aims 'to please and benefit my reader'.[8] Greek scholars have debated for a century, with some uneasiness and widely differing judgment, what place to assign to the *School* in the canon of Rhigas's work. The debate has ranged from the view expressed in 1892 that it was 'a youthful aberration' to the most recent view that it has a serious social relevance.[9] Its conjunction in the same year with the *Anthology* has been held to indicate that political freedom and freedom of enquiry are intimately related.[10] The implications of the *School*, however, are more daring and reflect a more advanced stage of the Greek Enlightenment than the morally neutral implications of the *Anthology*.

In judging both Rhigas's intention and the degree of his success, it must be remembered that the six stories are only a minute fraction of Rétif's enormous output, most of which was far from moral in its implications. Rétif's reputation was virtually that of a pornographer, so Rhigas's range of choice was limited, especially as he had only four out of 42 volumes at his disposal. It was clearly intentional that he chose stories which all concerned romances between young people of widely differing social class.[11] In each of the first two ('The young Provincial' and 'The workshop Apprentice') a boy of humble birth falls in love with the daughter of his employer; in each of the other four, a wealthy aristocrat honourably loves a poor girl. The social and economic obstacles to marriage are eventually overcome in every case except one ('La mort d'amour', or 'Death for Love' in Greek), which ends in the death of both lovers. In one other case ('First Love'), which had been partly autobiographical for Rétif, Rhigas alters the climax to produce a different ending of his own, though still a happy one.

All the stories emphasise moral, patriotic and educational values; but they were also trying to break, or at least to loosen, the bonds of puritanism. Both the brilliance and the dark shadows of pre-revolutionary France are made apparent, in a way which would remind Greek readers of the same characteristics in Phanariote society. Rhigas deliberately chose to adapt rather than to translate Rétif's stories word for word. If his success is judged incomplete, and the effect seems naive, it must be remembered that these six stories are the first example of romantic fiction in modern Greek.

There was a particular significance for Rhigas in each of the stories that he chose. In one of them ('First Love') Rousseau makes a personal appearance: it was chosen because Rousseau, along with Voltaire and Montesquieu, was one of the strongest French influences on Rhigas. In another ('The workshop Apprentice') mention is made of an account of the *Last Voyage of Captain Cook*, chosen because geographical exploration was a subject which fascinated Rhigas. Others emphasised the importance of hard work for fair wages, and of abstention from tobacco (especially for girls) and from sexual relations before marriage, or even 'forwardness' in the case of girls. For the Phanariotes especially there was the salutary lesson that all men are by nature equal, and that true nobility is rooted in the personality of man, not in the empty titles of ancestors.

To ridicule aristocratic pretensions, Rhigas chose one story ('The young Provincial') in which the snobbish grandmother of a wealthy heiress consents to her marriage with the humble hero only with extreme reluctance. A bizarre twist in the story wins her consent: she discovers that the youth had previously been married to his elderly employer, a woman of even higher status

34

than herself, who had promptly died three days later, leaving him a vast fortune. Even then the class-conscious old lady insists that a clause should be included in the marriage contract binding the low-born youth never to address his wife in the second person singular. Such was the society of pre-1789 France which Rétif mocked; and such was the Phanariote society which Rhigas satirised.

Rétif suited him well as a model, both because he was a self-educated writer and because he wrote on the eve of the French Revolution. But like Rétif, Rhigas did not regard the society which he satirised with unmixed contempt. It was, after all, at Bucharest that he had served his own cultural apprenticeship. He garnished Rétif's stories with a wide selection of romantic poems, mostly drawn from popular Phanariote works of the day;[12] and at least some of his aristocratic types are humane in outlook. The depiction of a quasi-Phanariote society is thus merged in the primary purpose of what Rhigas called 'philhellenism'—the moral and cultural regeneration of the Greeks.

His own philhellenism expressed itself most clearly in the choice of one story called, in both French and Greek, 'The new Pygmalion'. It relates the successful efforts of a noble Marquis to mould a poor orphan into a suitable wife, as Pygmalion formed his beautiful statue. By virtue of the title, the story gave Rhigas the opportunity for many footnotes on Greek legends and history. He explains the stories of not only Pygmalion and Galatea, but also Zeus and Kronos, Adonis, the Golden Age, the Furies, Mithridates and Pharnaces, and so on. He counsels a life of active service in contrast with the contemplative follies of Brahmins and fakirs. He describes the customs of the West in caring for orphans and educating girls in convent schools. He elaborates the lovers' dialogues, sometimes printing them as if for performance in the theatre, with stage directions not supplied by Rétif. Altogether, the narrative is a classic example of Rhigas's homely, moral and 'philhellenic' technique.

Patriotic footnotes also appear in other stories. Where Rétif wrote in 'Honour lost for Love' that Parisian girls were the most beautiful in the world, Rhigas, without altering the text, adds in a footnote:

In this I think, as a patriot, that the writer is mistaken; there are beautiful girls everywhere, and we have ours too. The beauty of Greek girls is proverbial to Europeans; wishing to describe a lovely creature, they say: 'Voilà une beauté Grecque!'[13]

These words give us a glimpse of Rhigas's sentimental development—using the word 'sentimental' in the sense of Sterne and Flaubert.

Rhigas's relations with women are almost a closed book. He never married; nothing that could be called a love affair is known in his life. Perdikaris implied that he was a libertine, but the only positive evidence is that he was once prosecuted for corrupting his mother's domestic servant at Bucharest.[14] The case was tried in an ecclesiastical court, which imposed only a minor penalty; so it was presumably a case of seduction rather than rape. But he was certainly a believer in the principle of feminist equality. He showed it emphatically later when he drafted his revolutionary programme; and he showed it more subtly in the preface to the *School of Delicate Lovers* and in later romantic publications.

The dedication of the *School* is addressed to 'sensitive young girls and boys'.[15] The girls are placed first, and the unusual word for 'sensitive' (*aisthantikes*) conveys the meaning of Sterne's 'sentiment'. In the preface, Rhigas emphasises that his book is a 'moral work', even if it deals with 'erotic material'. He defends this judgment by pointing out that 'the love affairs included in the present book end in marriage, which is a sacrament, so let not my critics waste their breath'. They did so, all the same, even if they did not notice that the *School of Delicate Lovers* was based on the work of the notorious pornographer Rétif de la Bretonne. None, probably, also noticed the interesting coincidence that Rhigas's *School* was published in the same year as the first performance in Vienna of Mozart's *Cosi fan tutte*, with its sub-title *The School for Lovers*.

Both the *Anthology of Physics* and the *School of Delicate Lovers* were printed and published in Vienna, where there were several presses licensed to print in Greek. The *Anthology* was printed at the Trattner press; the *School* at the press of Joseph von Baumeister, whose managers were two Greek brothers, George and Publius Markidis-Poulios. Rhigas did not use the Trattner press again, but his relations with the Poulios brothers became very close. Initially, perhaps, their friendship blossomed from the great success of the *School of Delicate Lovers*. The first edition was quickly sold out, and it was several times reprinted; before long the stories were translated into Romanian. A further bond between Rhigas and the Poulios brothers lay in the liberal and even revolutionary sympathies which they came to share.[16]

The two brothers had more than once applied for a licence to publish a Greek newspaper; so had other Greeks. As early as 1784 Baron von Herbert-Rathkeal, the Austrian Ambassador in Constantinople, had urged Chancellor von Kaunitz not to allow such a publication at all, at least for the time being, because it was sure to give offence to the Turkish authorities. In this he was unsuccessful, however; licences were granted to more than one publisher, though only for one newspaper at a time. The Poulios brothers' application was successful in 1790, after an earlier venture had failed. Their first issue came out on the last day of the year. The paper, called simply the *Ephimeris* [*Newspaper*], prospered and was widely read, not only by local Greeks but even by Turks as far afield as Vidin (no doubt including Pasvanoglou himself). On the whole, it seemed to upset the Austrian authorities more than the Turks, but fresh proposals to suppress it from time to time were unsuccessful until 1798.[17]

Rhigas was a subscriber to *Ephimeris* from the start, and continued to receive it after he left Vienna.[18] He had no directing or editorial role, but the paper became noticeably sympathetic to his views as they developed. This was especially the case after the Poulios brothers took over full control (though not ownership) of the press in 1792, when Baumeister took up his appointment at the Imperial Court. Five years later the press undertook the printing not only of Rhigas's literary works but of his revolutionary pamphlets as well.

Through the two brothers Rhigas formed also a close relationship with their colleague, George Vendotis from Zakynthos, who was an able scholar as well as a printer and publisher. It was he who had applied for the first licence which offended Rathkeal in 1784. He was engaged at the same time in editing a tri-lingual lexicon of French, Italian and Romaic (demotic Greek), which was published in 1790. Vendotis admired Rhigas and wrote an epigram to him which is printed in the *Anthology of Physics*.[19] Later he contributed to Rhigas's published translations and helped him with his great *Map of Hellas*. Perhaps his chief claim to be remembered is that he was the first to name his friend Pheraios rather than Velestinlis; but Rhigas never adopted the classical form himself because it reminded him painfully of Jason, the ancient tyrant of Pherai.[20] Although Vendotis became very close to Rhigas, he was probably never involved in any revolutionary activities, since he died in 1795.

The Poulios brothers, on the other hand, would almost certainly have shared Rhigas's tragic fate if they had not been Austrian rather than Ottoman subjects. At the beginning of the last decade of the eighteenth century the risks of liberalism in Vienna were not yet so great as they later became. Even the Austrian censorship was not excessively oppressive. In the case of Greek publications, the responsible official was Bartholomew Kospitar, a scholar in both Greek and Serbo-Croat, who was sympathetic to the subject nationalities. It was not until the growth of anti-Jacobinism in Austria, after the French began to export their revolution, that the Greeks and other minorities felt the pressure of a more suspicious régime. The turning-point was marked by the establishment in 1793 of a Ministry of Police and Home Affairs under Count von Pergen, with direct responsibility to the Emperor.

In 1790, with the war against Turkey approaching its end, there was a relative sense of freedom among the Greeks at Vienna. Rhigas, however, faced difficulties of another kind, as Baron von Langenfeld was proving an unsatisfactory employer. At first Rhigas treated him with almost exaggerated respect. His *Anthology of Physics*, for example, was fulsomely dedicated to 'the Right Honourable Langenfeld, Baron of the Roman Empire and Grand Sirdar, Kyrios [=Sir] Christodoulos Kirlian'.[21] The title, conferred on 16 August 1790, gives a *terminus post quem* for the *Anthology*. But Rhigas soon found Langenfeld a disloyal friend to the Greeks as well as a traitor to the Sultan.

Rhigas left Vienna for Bucharest in December 1790, stopping on the way at Herrmanstadt with Ioannis Mavroyenis. He then sued Langenfeld for arrears of pay, but Langenfeld counterclaimed that Rhigas had mishandled his funds. The case lasted a year in court, and the outcome is unknown.[22] A year later Langenfeld was engaged in another sordid case. On his information, two young Greeks, Ioannis Khatzimoschos and George Theocharis (the latter a close friend of Rhigas) were arrested and tried on charges of espionage during the recent war.[23] After detailed hearings in court, beginning in January 1793, the charges were dismissed. The two young men then started a counter-suit against Langenfeld. Again the outcome is unknown, but Langenfeld's reputation was permanently tarnished, and Rhigas severed all contact with him.

When Rhigas returned from Vienna to Bucharest, the war was over, though formal treaties of peace had not yet been signed between Turkey, Russia and Austria. Bucharest was evacuated by the Russian army during 1791, and a new Hospodar, Michael Soutzos, was appointed. Rhigas, who already knew Soutzos from his previous residence at Bucharest, became his secretary. Probably also he resumed his appointment as a part-time teacher at the Academy; possibly he became an interpreter at the French Consulate (though doubt was later cast on this appointment by the Austrian authorities). Since he did not give up his interests as a writer, editor and publisher, he was certainly fully occupied.

He also had a number of private activities, which are on record in the Romanian official archives.[24] Among them were the management of his property in the country, which he had owned at least since 1788. His home in a wealthy quarter of Bucharest involved him in local affairs: the supervision of a campaign against cholera in the district; the representation of his neighbourhood in a legal suit over the opening of a new road; and the conduct of a dispute with a local monastery. He was, in short, an established citizen. Besides, he had to look after his mother and Kostis, his younger brother, who were settled in Bucharest.

His commercial and official interests required some travelling between 1791 and 1796; but how much is doubtful. He was certainly at Trieste in 1794, since one of his portraits is dated there in that year.[25] According to some accounts, though positive evidence is lacking, he visited western Europe;[26] and others claim that he travelled, disguised as a dervish, to many parts of the

Ottoman Empire.[27] The latter story is no doubt mythical, but the alleged visits to the West are not impossible. They are said to have included Italy, Germany, France and (most improbably) England.[28] But it should be noted that the Romanian records confirm his presence at Bucharest at various dates throughout the years 1791–96. So his absences cannot have been very long; and it is certain that when Michael Soutzos was transferred from Bucharest in 1793, to become Hospodar of Moldavia, Rhigas did not accompany him.

During those years, Rhigas produced no new written work of his own. It has been suggested that he may have had a hand in a new collection of romantic novelettes called *Love's Consequences*, which was published at Vienna in 1792, apparently by his friend George Vendotis. Other authors have been suggested, including Athanasios Psalidas, a learned school-master who studied at Vienna, or Ioannis Karatzas, a young scholar from Cyprus who was to die with Rhigas. The work was clearly influenced by the *School of Delicate Lovers* in both style and themes. Its description on the title-page as 'a moral-erotic narrative . . . composed in the simple dialect' is closely modelled on that of the *School*.[29] These characteristics do not amount to evidence of Rhigas's authorship, but they do show that he had created a literary fashion which endured.

There was another very different publication of the same period in which it seems probable that he had a hand, though only as publisher and editor. This was the first printed edition of a religious homily called *The Prophecies of Agathangelos*, which had been circulating in manuscript for about forty years and had much influenced Greeks of all classes. The attribution of its publication to Rhigas was made by the editor of a later edition (1838) who called himself the *Zeloprophitis* or 'zealous prophet'. The title-page of the first edition bears the imaginary date 1279 and an equally imaginary place of publication, Agathoupolis. The book is generally assumed to have been printed and published at Vienna between 1790 and 1795.[30]

The nominal author of the *Prophecies*, Hieronymos Agathangelos, was supposedly a thirteenth-century monk, born in Rhodes and settled in Sicily. In reality the author was probably an Archimandrite on Mount Athos called Theoklitos Polyeidis, who wrote in about the 1750s. The work consists of ten chapters recording events from the thirteenth to the eighteenth centuries, but of course only the last part of the text contains actual 'prophecies'. Of these the most important is one to the effect that the Greeks would be liberated by a 'blond race' from the East, who would restore Constantinople as their capital. Naturally the 'blond race' was taken to be the Russians. It is probably correct to attribute the publication to Rhigas. If it had not been the case, then its authenticity would probably have been challenged when the edition of the *Zeloprophitis* appeared in 1838, for many of Rhigas's contemporaries were then still living. A minor defect was also, it must be said, characteristic of Rhigas, who had a habit of sending works to press too hastily. Comparison with the 1838 edition shows that he omitted a substantial section, overlapping chapters VII and VIII. This error suggests that he may not have been able to supervise the printing, having perhaps left the manuscript behind with the printer at Vienna when he returned to Bucharest early in 1791.

His motives for undertaking the publication are uncertain. It might be thought that it pleased him to see in Agathangelos a fellow-prophet, albeit one whose instincts were unsound. But monks and mysticism had little appeal to his positivistic temperament. He was always a loyal Orthodox Christian, but he did not try, as others did later, to use the Church as an actively revolutionary factor; nor did he any longer share the Greeks' traditional confidence in Russia as a liberator. Apart from his first introduction to the Russian Ambassador in Constantinople, if that story is true, his contacts with the Russians were slight. His hopes of liberation were already fastened exclusively on France. It has even been suggested that he made amendments to the *Prophecies* so that they might also be applicable to the French; but there is no positive evidence of such changes.[31]

It is true that the *Prophecies* contain a clear prediction of the downfall of the Austrian Empire, which might have been taken to be an interpolation by a Francophile editor. But it would have been extraordinarily reckless on Rhigas's part to have invented such a provocative and gratuitous challenge to the Austrian censorship. The publication of the *Prophecies* inevitably remains something of an anomaly in his literary output. Perhaps the simplest explanation is right, that he undertook it for a straight commercial reason, to make a profit from a potential best-seller.

A few years later, when he published his maps of Moldavia and Vallachia, it was for exactly that reason. When he gave this explanation to his Austrian interrogators in 1798, they noted simply that 'there is nothing to show otherwise'.[32] There is nothing also to show otherwise in the case of the *Prophecies*. Rhigas was, when all is said and done, always a businessman.

◦ ◦ ◦

[1] Enepekidis (1965), 49–51; Laios (1955), 3–9.
[2] Xénopol, II. 286.
[3] Daskalakis (1937), 9–10.
[4] Rhigas, *Anthology of Physics* (1790), 176; Vranousis (1953), 287.
[5] Thomopoulos, 1028-38; Pistas (1971), xxiii-xxv.
[6] Rhigas, *op. cit.* (n. 4), vi–ix; Vranousis (1953), 261.
[7] Rhigas, *op. cit.* (n. 4), 165 ff., Vranousis (1953), 286 ff.
[8] Pistas (1971), 1.
[9] *Ibid.*, xxxix–xlii; 229–33.
[10] *Ibid.*, xlv.
[11] *Ibid.*, xviii–xxv, for detailed analysis.
[12] *Ibid.*, xxvi–xxvii.
[13] *Ibid.*, 122, fn.; Vranousis (1953), 196, fn.
[14] Amantos (1948), 400; Oikonomidis, 135; Iorga (1900), 26–30.
[15] Pistas (1971), 1.
[16] Laios (1958), 202 ff.
[17] Laios (1961), 16–19; *idem* (1958), 247–60.
[18] Oikonomidis, 134; Iorga (1915), 35.
[19] Rhigas, *op. cit.* (n. 4), x; Vranousis (1953), 264.
[20] Amantos (1948), 396–7.
[21] Rhigas, *op. cit.* (n. 4), iii–x; Vranousis (1953), 261.
[22] Laios (1955), 3–9; Enepekidis (1956), 378–80.
[23] *Ibid.*, 382 ff.
[24] Oikonomidis, 135–6; Vranousis (1953), 35–8; *idem* (1980), 90–1.
[25] Lambros (1905), 635–7.
[26] Kordatos (1974), 49; 58.
[27] Mikhalopoulos (1930), 54.
[28] Ubicini, VIII (1881), 243.
[29] Vranousis (1953), 216 ff., reprinting two stories from this collection.
[30] A. Politis (1969), 173–92.
[31] MEE, s.v. Rhigas.
[32] Legrand, 62–3.

IV

THE SEEDS OF EMANCIPATION

ON the surface, the years from 1791 to 1796 were a period of quiescence in Rhigas's life. But it was the quiescence of ripening seed. There was no new publication until the end of the period, and no revolutionary activity that can be identified. In sharp contrast, the last two years of his life, from the middle of 1796, were a period of almost frenetic activity, both with the pen and also, at least in intention, with the sword. Clearly the activity of those last years did not spring *ex nihilo*. It must have had its roots in the five preceding years.

The formal ending of the Austro-Turkish war by the Treaty of Sistov on 4 August 1791, followed five months later by that of the Russo-Turkish war by the Treaty of Yassy on 9 January 1792, seemed to inaugurate an era of general pacification in eastern Europe. But Rhigas was disillusioned with the imperialism of both Austria and Russia. His hopes lay even more than before with the French, and they were perhaps reinforced by the Francophile sympathies of his new employer, Michael Soutzos.

Soutzos had other confidential secretaries besides Rhigas. He may have tried to keep them insulated from each other, but they were all Greeks and several of them were friends. One was Dimitrakis Tournavitis, who had been close to Rhigas during his quarrel with Langenfeld at Vienna. Tournavitis was regarded by both the Turkish and the Austrian authorities as a dangerous intriguer. He was in touch with the French Consulate, and also acted as an adviser to Rhigas's friend Pasvanoglou. For these connections he paid with his life in 1798, at the hands of the Turks.

An important role in Soutzos's secretariat was played also by Panayotis Kodrikas, a less conspiratorial figure. He was clearly on familiar terms with Rhigas, since he tried to intervene in the high court at Bucharest to compel Langenfeld to settle his debt to Rhigas.[2] Through Kodrikas, Soutzos was in correspondence with the French diplomatic agent, Constantine Stamatis (by then known in Paris as Stamaty).

Stamaty was born at Constantinople and studied at Bucharest, but emigrated to France in 1764. He acquired French nationality, entered the diplomatic service, and served in the Danubian principalities, but was unacceptable to the Porte as Consul General. He reported to Soutzos through Kodrikas from many capitals—Paris, Vienna, Berlin and Warsaw—between 1791 and 1794.[3] It is reasonable to assume that Rhigas had access to his reports.

But Rhigas's service with Soutzos did not last long. Soutzos remained at Bucharest only from March 1791 to the end of 1792, after which he was transferred to Yassy as Hospodar of Moldavia. Rhigas did not accompany him; it was possibly after this date that he held an appointment as interpreter at the French Consulate. There he became particularly friendly with Émile Gaudin, who served at Bucharest from 1793 to 1797.[4] Gaudin had a Greek wife born on Naxos; he was regarded by both Austrian and Turkish officials as a trouble-maker on behalf of the Greeks and a spy-master for the French. For Rhigas his value was as a provider of access to French sources of information and publications. One of these sources was still Stamaty, who published an open news-letter in Paris from 1792. It was now a very different western world on which Rhigas had a distant but distinct outlook, for towards the end of his first residence in Bucharest there had occurred in 1789 the most unforgettable event of the eighteenth century in Europe.

During his first residence at Bucharest (1789–90), his inspiration had been the French Enlightenment. Hence the *School of Delicate Lovers*, the *Anthology of Physics*, and the abortive plan to translate *L'Esprit des Lois*. His literary and intellectual models were Montesquieu, Rousseau, Fontenelle, Barthélemy, and even Rétif de la Bretonne. In the second period (1791–6), his inspiration was the French Revolution; but in this case his models are less easily identifiable. They might have been Condorcet, Sieyès, Mirabeau, Chénier; they could hardly have been Danton, Marat, St Just, Robespierre.

Seen from eastern Europe, the French Revolution was already showing ambiguous symptoms. The early stages had been exhilarating for a Democratic Republican (the two terms are synonymous in Greek). The French had abolished the feudal system (1789), the titles of nobility (1790), the monarchy (1792), and the Catholic hierarchy (1793). But in April 1792 France had

44

plunged into war with Austria, and with Prussia soon afterwards. Also in that April, Rouget de Lisle had published the *Marseillaise*, a song after Rhigas's own heart which he must have longed to imitate. A so-called 'Greek Marseillaise' has been commonly attributed to him, but not with certainty.[5]

Even while the war was in progress, there was still some good news from Paris. Slavery was abolished in the French colonies (1794), and freedom of the press was established in France (1796). Successive constitutions were drafted in 1789, 1791, 1793, 1795, though none of them took practical effect. For Greeks hoping for liberation, however, there was also more shocking news. In 1793–94, the French Revolution turned into the 'Terror', of which Korais and other Greeks in Paris wrote fearful accounts. First Louis XVI and then his Queen, Marie Antoinette, were executed on the guillotine. So were thousands of others, against whom no charges were proved. Soon Britain, Spain and Holland joined Prussia and Austria in the First Coalition against France. At first it seemed that the Revolution must be crushed; then an amazing series of victories was won by the French. By 1795 the First Coalition was disintegrating, but by 1796 the war of self-defence had turned into a war of French aggression.

Rhigas was shaken by some of these developments, and he misunderstood others. He interpreted them in terms of their implications for Greek liberation, but it was unclear what those implications would be. Because the fate of the Greeks had been determined for many centuries by the impact of the great powers' conflicting interests, they have had a persistent weakness for supposing that Greece is the central focus of the powers' foreign policies. Rhigas was not immune from this delusion, as he was to show in 1796–97; but during his last five years at Bucharest (1791–96) he was more cautious. He confined himself at first to his official and commercial business, and to educational and literary preparations for the emancipation of his people. He did not yet take a headlong leap into revolution.

But independence was constantly in his thoughts. He saw that it would never come peacefully, but also that it would never be consolidated without a moral and cultural foundation. The foundation would take longer to prepare than the final uprising, which he imagined would be short and decisive. Like Adamantios Korais, who lived in Paris throughout the French Revolution, Rhigas saw that the cultural emancipation of the Greeks would be long and arduous. Korais thought that it would take until the middle of the nineteenth century; Rhigas was more optimistic and more impatient. Korais, who had spent all his adult life in western Europe, appeared to believe that independence would come about in some inexplicable way as an automatic result of educational maturity. Rhigas, who had spent his youth under Ottoman rule, saw that it would never come without an armed rebellion.

A lithograph of, from left to right, Adamantios Korais, Rhigas Pheraios and Alexander Ypsilantis, executed and printed at the expense of G. K. Ieropoulos and Brothers, in Lyon 1849 (National Historical Museum, Athens).

His instinct told him that education and revolution must advance in step; it was only their direction that caused him uncertainty. In the early 1790s he began his activities in both fields, all of which came to a climax in 1796–97. On the one hand, he sought to widen his compatriots' pride in their history and their understanding of the western enlightenment: they must undergo a social, moral, intellectual regeneration. On the other hand, he began testing the sympathies of Greeks of all classes, wherever they were to be found. These two tasks were now his mission in life.

The contacts which he had formed in Vienna as well as in Bucharest prepared the ground for both tasks. A central role in Vienna was played by the Poulios brothers, as printers, publishers and propagandists. Their *Ephimeris* was becoming boldly democratic and pro-French. At Constantinople it was persistently criticised by Rathkeal, and even by Constantine Ypsilantis (the son of Alexander, and once Rhigas's fellow-student), when he became Dragoman of the Porte in 1796.[6] Through their contacts abroad, the Poulios brothers were able to obtain and transmit to Rhigas foreign publications, including revolutionary French journals. He had a similar facility through the French Consulate at Bucharest. In these ways, although spasmodically and irregularly, he was introduced to more significant writers and thinkers than Rétif de la Bretonne.

At the same time he was drawing round himself a circle of friends, both at Vienna and at Bucharest, with whom discussion of liberation gradually passed from theoretical to practical ideas. His circle included merchants and their clerks, schoolmasters, academics and students, poets, manual workers and peasants. Most of them, particularly the merchants, had close contacts with their families and friends still living in Greece. The merchants at Vienna had already shown their patriotism by financing the privateering ships launched by Lambros Katsonis from Trieste during the Austro-Turkish war. They had also formed a delegation to approach Catherine the Great for support in 1790, though with little immediate success.[7] Presumably Rhigas kept in touch with these supporters at Vienna through occasional visits, ostensibly on commercial business, as well as by correspondence.

There were also Austrian, Hungarian and German sympathisers, if only a handful: Dr Peter Frank, who regularly treated the Greeks of Vienna free of charge; Kaspar Peters, a teacher of French; Joseph Baumeister and J. C. Engel, and a few others. But these men were not natural revolutionaries; they could contribute little more than sympathy and financial help. Another non-Greek ally, at least potentially, was a much more formidable character: Osman Pasvanoglou, Rhigas's friend since 1789, who led a vigorous rebellion against the Sultan from 1793 to 1796.

It is well-nigh impossible to disengage Pasvanoglou's relations with Rhigas from legend. Whether they were in touch during those years is quite uncertain. It was certainly a possibility while Rhigas was at Bucharest, through his colleague Tournavitis, if not more directly. But if they were in touch, it had no immediate consequences for the Greeks. Pasvanoglou's rebellion ended in deadlock. Unable to crush him, the Sultan granted him a free pardon and even a high honour. Pasvanoglou remained passive until December 1797, the month of Rhigas's own fatal initiative; but again there is no positive evidence that action was concerted between them.[8]

It has been suggested that when Pasvanoglou agreed to an armistice with the Sultan's forces in 1796, Rhigas helped to bring about a reconciliation by drafting his statement of self-justification for him.[9] This seems like an echo of the encounter between them in 1789, when Rhigas supposedly advised Pasvanoglou to consult him whenever the Sultan wrote critical letters, so that he could help in drafting the replies. Such stories bear the stamp of legend. Nevertheless, Rhigas could well have known much of what was going on behind the scenes. The affair could at least have provided him with useful new links, since Tournavitis, who was certainly in touch with Pasvanoglou, had a brother, Michael, living in Trieste; and among Michael Tournavitis's close friends were two merchants, Nicholas Plastaras and Paraschos Katsaros, who were both to become involved in Rhigas's later venture. Such personal links with Rhigas's future plans are shadowy but also substantial. It can only be conjectured what plans the rebellion of Pasvanoglou helped to stimulate in his head.

At Bucharest Rhigas's contacts consisted mainly in the renewal of acquaintances from his former years of residence. They were writers and intellectuals rather than revolutionaries. One of the most influential of them, however, was Dimitrios Katartzis, who took part fortuitously in an encounter which had fateful consequences. In 1793 Rhigas brought to visit him a young Greek called Christopher Perrhaivos, his own future biographer. Perrhaivos described the impression made on him by the old scholar's 'wise indoctrination', which determined him 'from that hour to share the struggle and the danger on behalf of his country'.[10]

Perrhaivos, who was then twenty years old, soon began to play a significant part in Rhigas's life and activity. Such is his own account of their relationship, on which Perrhaivos is himself the only first-

48

hand source. But he was not a boastful man, and his later contribution to the War of Independence in 1821 is evidence enough of his loyalty and courage. His origin is obscure, for he liked to create mysteries about himself. He was not born at Parga, as he later claimed for reasons of expediency,[11] but probably in Thessaly, not far from Rhigas's own birth-place. A hostile pamphlet about him claimed that he was the illegitimate son of a Jew and a Christian mother; but although he was almost certainly illegitimate, the rest of the story is false. His father was probably a monk called Jeremiah, who was an official of the cathedral at Larisa. Certainly it was Jeremiah who brought him up, and sent him to study medicine at Bucharest in 1793.[12] There he soon heard of Rhigas's celebrity, and quickly formed an admiring attachment to him.

Rhigas was sixteen years his senior, but he counted even younger men among his revolutionary associates in Vienna. At Bucharest Perrhaivos was probably the youngest, and also the most devoted. Perhaps because he was a medical student, and was Rhigas's only companion when he was arrested, the Austrian authorities exaggerated the degree to which Rhigas's support depended on 'students of medicine at foreign universities'.[13] They recognised, however, that local Greek merchants were also 'infected'. The fact is that numerically by far the widest range of Rhigas's contacts was among the Greek merchants in many cities, initially through his own commercial interests and probably in many cases only through correspondence.

During the interrogations of himself and his associates in 1798, it emerged that merchants and their employees amounted to about half the total of nearly a hundred names. That figure is probably an underestimate, since many of his contacts are not categorised by occupation in the interrogation reports. The merchants were variously located in Vienna, Pest, Trieste, Semlin, Constantinople, Smyrna, Bucharest, Yassy, Ioannina, Preveza. It was partly to account for this wide distribution that Rhigas was supposed to have travelled widely, often in disguise; but that is an improbable and unnecessary assumption. It seems unlikely that he ever set foot in Smyrna, Ioannina, or Preveza; and he was only in Semlin on his last tragic journey to his death at Belgrade. So far as the positive evidence goes, he never returned to Constantinople after his departure in 1786.

In any case, these were not the limits of his contacts further afield. Through Trieste, which he certainly visited, he could communicate with Italy and mainland Greece. Overland, he was in touch with Macedonia, Epiros and Thessaly through his own and his friends' family connections. Northwards, through fellow-merchants and sympathisers, he could communicate with Leipzig, Berne, Brussels, Amsterdam and Paris. None of these channels came into existence for revolutionary purposes, but only in the course of business. It was an imperceptible evolution which turned them to clandestine purposes in 1796.

On 1 August of that year Rhigas returned from Bucharest to Vienna, accompanied by Perrhaivos. Three days later the Austrian Consul in Bucharest reported Rhigas's departure to his Ministry of Foreign Affairs. He added that Rhigas intended to publish in Vienna 'a kind of Greek geographical map'; he also stressed Rhigas's close relations with Gaudin at the French Consulate.[14] Both Gaudin and Rhigas were therefore already regarded with suspicion at Vienna. Only a few weeks later, in September 1796, a group of Rhigas's friends heard him sing for the first time his famous *Thourios*, an unmistakably revolutionary composition.[15]

Rhigas never denied under interrogation that he often sang the *Thourios* and played the tune on his flute. By November 1796, the Austrians already had secret reports of contacts between the French and Greeks in Paris.[16] These reports did not yet implicate Rhigas by name. But they did give the name of a certain N. Polyzois as a source. Almost certainly this was the Dr Polyzos (also called Polyzoidis) who was named elsewhere as an associate of Rhigas. It can be assumed that he was a quite unconscious source—an example of the lack of caution with which Rhigas's associates conducted their affairs throughout. It was clear, in any case, that the movement had already begun.

Vienna was a less easy-going capital in 1796 than when Rhigas had left it five years earlier. The effects on Austria of the French Revolution were already apparent. The war begun in 1792 was going badly for the Austrians, who had already lost most of their territory in northern Europe. The Terror in France had induced a deep fear of Jacobinism, especially after the execution in 1793 of the King, and especially that of Marie Antoinette, who was the aunt of the reigning Austrian Emperor, Francis II. There was even a threat of revolution within the Austrian Empire in 1795, led by the Hungarian Professor Ignace-Joseph Martinovicz, who was known to have French acquaintances. The fact that he had formerly been a trusted adviser of the Austrian Emperor only increased the disquiet. His conspiracy, which aimed to introduce a republican constitution, ended with his execution in 1795. There naturally followed an increase in Count von Pergen's secret police.

It may be doubted whether these developments caused Rhigas any immediate concern. He had not returned to Vienna with plans for an early revolution, but chiefly to carry out a number of literary and publishing projects. The press controlled by the Poulios brothers was the natural place to put his plans into effect. His projects were still primarily educational in purpose, partly to instil in the Greeks a pride in their history and ancestry, and partly to enlarge their awareness of European civilisation. In some cases his plans were bound to stimulate hostility to their Ottoman oppressors, and might therefore be regarded as seditious. But Rhigas had not yet reached the stage of drafting revolutionary proclamations or a programme for independence.

More than half a dozen projects were in hand, or in his head, when he arrived in Vienna. Three of them were purely literary: a translation from Italian of Metastasio's drama in verse, the *Olympia*; a translation from French of Marmontel's romantic story, 'The Shepherdess of the Alps'; and a translation from German of Salomon Gessner's poem, 'The First Sailor'. These three works were published together under the title of *The Moral Tripod*, by the Poulios press in 1797.

The next project, published by the same press in the same year, was a work of historical imagination. It was a translation from French of volume IV of *The Voyage of the Young Anacharsis* by the Abbé Barthélemy, which had enjoyed a great success when first published at Paris in 1788. A separate group of Rhigas's projects was a series of maps. There was one each of Moldavia and Vallachia; but much more important was a set of twelve maps on a larger scale under the overall title: *Map of Hellas, including its islands and a part of its numerous colonies in Europe and Asia*

Engraving of title-sheet of Rhigas's *Map of Hellas*
(archives of C. M. Woodhouse).

Detail of neighbouring sheet of Rhigas's *Map of Hellas* showing part of
Thessaly including Rhigas's birthplace and Pelion, Mount Athos
and northern Euboea.

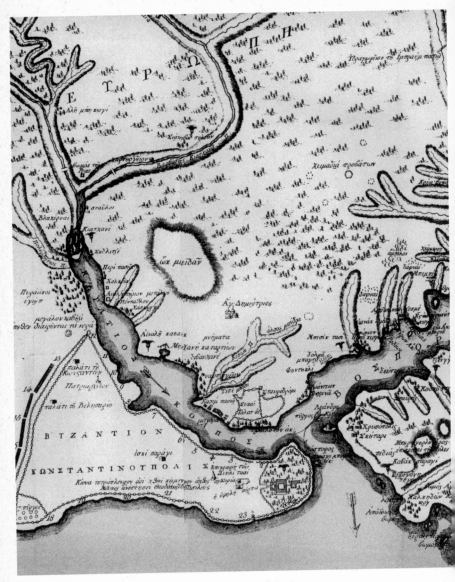

Detail of another sheet of Rhigas's *Map of Hellas* showing Constantinople, the Golden Horn and part of the Bosphoros.

Minor. The final project was an engraving of a head of Alexander the Great. All of these were published in 1797, except for the first sheet of the *Map of Hellas* which was published in 1796.[17] Both the maps and the Alexander are described as 'published for the benefit of Greeks and Philhellenes'.

Rhigas later gave, under interrogation, interesting statistics of the scale and distribution of these productions.[18] He had 900 copies of *The Moral Tripod* from the Poulios press, and 1,000 copies of *Anacharsis* vol. IV from another printer, the Pichler press. He had 1,220 copies of the twelve-sheet *Map of Hellas*, which was engraved by Franz Müller, printed by Jacob Nitsch; and an unspecified number of the maps of Moldavia and Vallachia, also by Müller and Nitsch. Finally, he had 1,200 copies of the engraving of Alexander the Great produced by the same two collaborators.

Of the distribution, he said that he delivered to two Bucharest merchants, Pilizakis and Avramis, both of whom were in Vienna at the time, 120 and 300 copies respectively of *The Moral Tripod*; and he later sent 700 copies of the same work to a merchant named George Michael at Yassy. The rest he distributed to various other agents. He sold 25 copies of *Anacharsis* vol. IV to a close associate, Evstratios Argentis, for 1000 florins to cover the cost of production, and sent 200 more through Argentis to Trieste, intending to pick them up later himself; and he delivered 500 copies to George Michael when he was at Vienna. He sent 624 copies of the complete twelve-sheet *Map of Hellas* through Argentis to Smyrna, and delivered 300 more to Pilizakis at Vienna.

He gave no details on the maps of Moldavia and Vallachia beyond saying that they were a 'speculative enterprise', subsidised by the respective Hospodars of the two provinces, Alexander Kallimakis and Alexander Ypsilantis. He distributed the portrait of Alexander the Great to Greeks at Vienna, also in unspecified numbers, and sent the surplus to Avramis at Bucharest to sell at 20 kreuzers each. These particulars show how simple and wide-ranging were Rhigas's means of commercial communication, which could be adapted to other purposes without arousing suspicion. They also show, since he was able to give the figures out of his head a year later, that he was a practical businessman.

Clearly it was impossible for all these projects to have been put in hand only after Rhigas returned to Vienna in August 1796, and published during 1797. Since all his collaborators were based in Vienna, they presumably at work under his direction before his arrival. His personal contribution to the projects is not in all cases certain. A few of the translations were his, but in the main his role was probably that of editor and publisher. There is no reason to doubt (though it has been questioned) that he himself drew the *Map of Hellas*, for cartography was his lifelong enthusiasm. For the rest, there are some uncertainties.

In *The Moral Tripod*, his name appears only in the dedication. Greek scholars are divided about his role in the three translations.[19] A prose version of Metastasio's *Olympia* in his own handwriting survives, but the published verse translation was probably not his work. It is generally agreed that the translation of Marmontel's 'Shepherdess' is not his own, but the translator cannot be identified. The translator of Gessner's 'First Sailor' is named on its title-page as Antonios Koronios, a young merchant at Trieste who was to die with Rhigas. His translation is in prose, but it was later put into verse by Rhigas himself. It is clear at least that he had an editorial hand in the complete work.

All three works in *The Moral Tripod* were chosen to illustrate moral themes, especially true love and womanly virtue. Two of them had the additional attraction of a Greek setting. In *Olympia* the celebrated Games play a significant part, which enabled Rhigas to include in his preface a list of the different contests, and also to draw attention to the relevant sheets of his *Map of Hellas*.[20] In the 'First Sailor' the hero wins his bride by swimming, with the support of a tree-trunk, across the strait between the Mani in the southern Peloponnese and the island of Cythera (Cerigo). This feat was presented as the beginning of navigation, which could thus be claimed as a Greek discovery, like so much else.

'The Shepherdess of the Alps' is a love-story which might well belong to the *School of Delicate Lovers*. It has the same didactic purpose, even down to an explanation of the Alps as 'the mountains which separate France from Italy'. The moral purpose is also the same. The story pairs a young aristocrat, who disguises himself as a peasant, with a humble maiden, who turns out to be of noble birth. Rhigas was an incurable romantic, and he rightly assumed that other Greeks shared his tastes. As he wrote in the preface to the *School*, his object was to combine instruction with enjoyment.

The translation of *Anacharsis* had a more frankly propagandist object. Barthélemy's immensely popular work was a fictitious but scholarly account of Greece in the fourth century BC, as seen through the eyes of a young Scythian prince. Anacharsis was a genuinely historical figure, once known as one of the Seven Sages and more recently identified by Rousseau as the 'noble savage'. The *Voyage* had already gone through three editions, and had grown from five volumes to seven. It was the second edition of 1789 which was used by Rhigas.[21]

The first three volumes had been translated by Rhigas's friend, the poet George Sakellarios, and published by the Poulios brothers. Volume IV, which alone survives, was in part translated by George Vendotis and in part by Rhigas himself.[22] Rhigas undertook chapters XXXV-XXXIX, including Anacharsis' account of Thessaly and also the chapter on Elis and the Olympic Games. This served to illustrate, as he pointed out, the translation in *The Moral Tripod* of Metastasio's *Olympia*. He also began, but never completed, a translation of volume VII of Anacharsis with the help of Dimitrios Nikolidis, a medical teacher born in Epiros, who was also, like Koronios, to share his fate in 1798.

Rhigas again emphasised the inter-connection of his literary and cartographical projects by reference to the *Anacharsis* in his *Map of Hellas*. Nine of the twelve sheets contain annotations referring to Barthélemy's work. Apart from the plan of Constantinople and the diagram of the Serai, the *Map of Hellas* was based on an atlas by Barbié du Bocage which accompanied the third French edition of *Anacharsis* (1791). But Rhigas's twelve sheets contain much more than cartographical detail.[23] They include commentaries on historic sites, battles and other events: for example, Simonides' famous epigram on Thermopylai, and a couplet from Sophocles on Rhigas's birth-place at Pherai. There are also drawings of 162 coins, mostly taken from publications of classical Greek coinage, but also including six Byzantine coins on the sheet depicting Constantinople. One of these six is a coin of the last Emperor, Constantine XI Palaiologos, with the legend:

'Gold, and we were enslaved'. Round the outer margin of the whole set runs a series of names of historic leaders, among them the Macedonian Kings, the Roman and Byzantine Emperors, and even the Ottoman Sultans from 1453 to his own day.

Undeniably, the twelve sheets were provocative as propaganda, because they depicted Hellas as including the territories of Albania, Serbia, Bulgaria, and western Anatolia, using Greek names wherever possible. It has been argued that the map had a further purpose: it was designed for use in a military campaign.[24] If this were true, then an even more provocative intention should be noted. It was stated at the time by J. C. Engel, who knew Rhigas personally, that the series of maps was to comprise eventually twenty-four sheets in all.[25] This was double the number actually published; so in which direction were the additional twelve to have extended? It could hardly have been northwards, not only because Rhigas was already preparing maps of Moldavia and Vallachia on a different scale, but also because a northward extension would encroach on Austrian territory as well, which could hardly be treated as part of Hellas on a map to be published at Vienna. The natural assumption is that the extension would have been to the east, and perhaps the south: in other words, it would have embraced most of the Ottoman Empire. This assumption accords with the implications of Rhigas's *Thourios*, which was taking its final form at the same date. The *Thourios* was a call to arms not only of the Greeks but of all the other oppressed nationalities in the Empire: in Europe, the Bulgars, Albanians, Bosnians, Macedonians, Montenegrins, Romanians, and 'Christian brothers from the Sava and the Danube'; in Asia, the Turks, Armenians, Georgians, Arabs, and 'men of the Black Sea'; in Africa, the Egyptians and negroes (*arapides*).[26]

No doubt the Austrian authorities took little note of Engel's first volume when it was published in 1797. But even as published, the *Map of Hellas* had disturbing implications for them as well as for the Ottoman authorities. Rhigas's friend Argentis, who had contributed to the cost of publishing *Anacharsis*, later admitted under interrogation that both that work and the maps were produced with the purpose of 'liberating the Morea' (Peloponnese).[27]

The two maps of Moldavia and Vallachia, which were en-

58

graved from originals by Austrian cartographers, were less questionable. Each was dedicated to the contemporary Hospodar of the province depicted, each of whom had helped to subsidise the publication. Neither map contained any implied threat of Greek aggrandisement or revolution. The Austrian authorities accepted Rhigas's statement that they had been published purely as a commercial transaction.[28] His series of pictorial productions in 1797 ended, however, with another example which could be regarded as having provocative implications.

This was an engraved portrait head of Alexander the Great. It was not based, as was once supposed, on a seal in the Imperial Museum at Vienna, but on a drawing published in 1749 from a different seal in a private collection.[29] As in the original, Rhigas, or his illustrator, surrounded the head with portraits of four of Alexander's successors (Ptolemy, Cassander, Antigonus and Seleucus), among whom his empire was eventually carved up. A short biography of Alexander was also added, together with scenes from his major battles. Since most of these battles were fought on what had become Ottoman territory, there was clearly an implied challenge to the Greeks to become worthy of their illustrious forebear.

For Rhigas as an educator of his compatriots, there were other points of significance. Alexander had been a pupil of Aristotle; and the birth-place of each of them (Pella and Stageira) was marked on his *Map of Hellas*. Alexander had been a great explorer as well as a great conqueror; and geography was Rhigas's favourite study. Alexander had been accompanied on his expedition by scientists—a pioneering example which was to be copied by Napoleon Bonaparte, who was already engaged in conquering northern Italy. Alexander was also a believer in supranationalism, which was the basic principle of Rhigas's future constitution.

In 1797 the Austrian authorities probably regarded all these publications as mere eccentricities. At least there was no intervention by the censors. For those who did not know Rhigas personally, it was still possible to regard him as no more than an enthusiastic publicist with an inflated opinion of himself. Certainly some of his conduct was curious. He was to be seen walking the streets of Vienna wearing a helmet and a Turkish robe, or alternatively a Vlach costume.[30] He made no secret of his ambitions for

The engraving of the head of Alexander the Great, published by Rhigas
in 1797 (National Historical Museum, Athens).

Greek independence. It is said that his peculiar costume attracted the attention of the Emperor Francis II, to whom he took the opportunity of lamenting the condition of the Greek people.[31] The Emperor is said to have responded 'with words full of sympathy'; but the story must be doubted, for Francis did not share the liberal sympathies of his father, Leopold II, whom he succeeded in 1792.

It must at least be assumed that Rhigas would not have been so foolish as to reveal what was actually going through his mind at the end of 1796. It was no longer a time simply for educational reform; it was no longer even a time for revolutionary songs. What made the difference at the turn of the year 1796–97 was the advance of Napoleon's army across northern Italy, which was putting into Rhigas's mind ideas unfit for Austrian ears. When he moved from Bucharest to Vienna, Napoleon had recently won his first major victory over the Austrian army at Lodi, and had occupied Milan. In the second half of 1796 the battle-lines in Italy hardly changed, but no one doubted that Napoleon would reach the Adriatic in the following spring.

Rhigas was instinctively pro-French, but he did not want to see Austria defeated and humiliated. What he wanted, like every Greek, was to see French arms turned away from central Europe and against the Ottoman Empire. The transition in his mind from plans for cultural emancipation to plans for revolution by force of arms was not instantaneous, nor did it depend solely on the prospect of French victories in Italy. Still, it is possible to detect a symbolic watershed in the month of September 1796. It was then that he sang his *Thourios* for the first time in the house of his friend Argentis, in the presence of five other sympathisers.[32] Their names were Dr Polyzos, Adam Mizanis, Markos Sevastos, Andreas Masoutis, and Constantine Amoiros, the last two being clerks in the employment of Argentis. Of the six, perhaps only Polyzos and Argentis were conscious revolutionaries; Masoutis and Amoiros ended by becoming renegades and informers. Such were the risks and weaknesses of conspiracy. The occasion was nevertheless historic in the sense that the *Thourios* combined Rhigas's two strongest aspirations: one literary, for the poem was his finest work of art; and one revolutionary, because it is the most complete and succinct expression of his intentions. By itself, the *Thourios* owed little to the hopes which were to be pinned on Napoleon, whose advance was stalled at that date on the line of Verona–Mantua. It addressed no appeal to the French, and looked only to the east and the south for allies. But in the following year, when Napoleon's advance accelerated to reach the outskirts of Venice and to penetrate Austria itself, Rhigas's aspirations took a new turn. They changed from aspirations into plans.

○ ○ ○

[1] Vranousis (1953), 38, 55.
[2] Oikonomidis, 134.
[3] Lair/Legrand, 25–79; 83–119.
[4] Vranousis (1953), 39, 55.
[5] See p.66-7 below.
[6] Laios (1958), 212.
[7] Vranousis (1953), 30–1.
[8] *Ibid.*, 53–7.
[9] Philemon (1834), 91 n. (a).
[10] Perrhaivos (1860), 12.
[11] *Ibid.*, 25 and fn.
[12] *Ibid.*, i-ii.
[13] Amantos (1930), 28–9.
[14] Vranousis (1953), 48; Camariano-Cioran (1970), 251–60.
[15] Legrand, 76–7.
[16] *Ibid.*, 2–7.
[17] See Daskalakis (1937), 9–20, for bibliographical details.
[18] Legrand, 60–3.
[19] For differing conjectures, see: Amantos (1930), 21; Daskalakis (1937), 13–15; Vranousis (1953), 295–9; Pistas (1971), 21; Dimaras (1974), 167–8.
[20] Rhigas, *Moral Tripod*, 3-6; Vranousis (1953), 302–3.
[21] Pantazopoulos, 16–17 and n. 54; Daskalakis (1937), 14–15.
[22] Rhigas, *Anacharsis*, IV (1799), chs. 35–9; Vranousis (1953), 329–57 (incomplete).
[23] Laios (1960), 231 ff.
[24] Enepekidis, *Vima*, 3 November 1953; Manessis (1962), 87 n. 31.
[25] Engel, I, 473–4.
[26] Rhigas, *Thourios*, lines 45–6; 63–8; 71–4.
[27] Amantos (1930), 84–5.
[28] Legrand, 62-5; Laios (1960), 286–9.
[29] Laios (1960), 292.
[30] Theotokis, 37; Enepekidis (1965), 75.
[31] Theotokis, 37; Enepekidis (1965), 73; Mikhalopoulos, 39.
[32] Legrand, 76–7.

V

TEXTS OF REVOLUTION

O N 20 February 1797 the *Ephimeris* announced that the *Map of Hellas* would be published in April and May. Readers were urged to order copies in good time, because the publisher would be leaving Vienna after May; and Argentis later testified, under interrogation, that Rhigas had intended to leave for Greece six months earlier than he eventually did, which was in December.[1] But he would hardly have advertised an intention to go to Greece so openly. In February, his plan was not yet formulated, for much depended on Napoleon, whose army in Italy was still immobilised by winter. It was not in fact until July that Rhigas made even his first attempt to contact Napoleon; and he was then still at Vienna.[2]

If he hoped to secure French support for a Greek revolution, he had to have something to show them that he was a worthwhile partner. The literary and pictorial publications which he had seen through the press in the early months of 1797 could be seen as a contribution to long-term indoctrination, but what he now needed to prepare was undisguised propaganda. For this purpose Rhigas was engaged, in the summer of 1797, on compositions of an entirely new kind. They were embodied in two pamphlets, which were to be printed at the Poulios press.

No printed copies of either work survive, although 3,000 copies were printed of the one and 1,000 of the other.[3] The earlier was known for short as the *New Political Order*, but was confusingly called by the Austrian police the *Revolutionary Proclamation*, which was the title only of the first item contained in it. The second was loosely known as the *Military Manual* though again this was the title only of one item in it. All 1,000 printed copies of the *Military Manual* were seized by the Austrian police at the press, together with the manuscript, and all were destroyed. Some 215 out of the 3,000 copies of the *New Political Order* escaped seizure and destruction by the Austrian police, but all were presumably lost or destroyed by those who received them.[4] On the other hand, the Austrian authorities made a German translation of much of the *New Political Order*, which survives; and so do two manuscripts in Greek, neither of them by Rhigas himself.[5] Greek scholars have had considerable success in reconstructing this pamphlet, and even some degree of success in reconstructing the *Military Manual*. According to an Austrian employee of the Poulios press, the *New Political Order* was printed under Rhigas's own supervision during two nights about five weeks before Christmas 1797.[6] It had been several months in preparation. The full title was the *New Political Order of the Inhabitants of Roumeli, Asia Minor, the Mediterranean Islands and Vlachobogdania*. By 'Roumeli' was evidently meant the whole Balkan area south of the Danube; 'Vlachobogdania' meant the Danubian principalities. The scope of the *New Political Order* was therefore roughly equivalent to the extent of the twelve sheets of the *Map of Hellas* together with the two maps of Vallachia and Moldavia.

The text comprised four items.[7] First, there was the 'Revolutionary Proclamation', with the sub-title 'In defence of the laws and the fatherland'. Between the lines of the sub-title was placed, horizontally, the club of Herakles surmounted by three crosses; and along the club were written the words 'freedom, equality, brotherhood'. The formulation was roughly similar to Rhigas's seal, as decribed by Kalaphatis and Perrhaivos. The second and third items were the 'Rights of Man', in 35 articles, and the 'Constitution of the Hellenic Republic', in 124 articles, both based on French models. The fourth and last item was the *Thourios*, which was already known but not previously printed.

The *Military Manual* is more problematic.[8] It seems to have comprised two main items and two poems. First came what could properly be called the 'military manual' itself, based on a work published in 1743 by the Austrian Field-Marshal Graf von Khevenhüller-Frankenburg (1683–1744) under the title *Kurzer Begriff aller Militärischen Operationen sowohl im Feld als Festungen* (*Concise Theory of all Military Operations both in the Field and against Fortresses*).[9] Rhigas evidently made a summary or adaptation of this work, possibly from a French translation made in 1771. Bound with this manual were two songs, which were described in the Austrian archives as being imitations of the French 'Carmagnole' and of a German song, 'Freut euch des

Lebens' ('Cherish ye Life'); and probably also an item called the 'Democratic Catechism', of which nothing more is known.

The title of the last item may have been suggested by the *Catéchisme français* of Poisson de la Chabeaussière, written to inculcate the principles of republican morality in school-children, which was translated into Greek in 1797. The reason for supposing that Rhigas's 'Catechism' formed part of the *Military Manual* lies in his statement, under interrogation in 1798, that he had received from Greece and copied out a 'ganz demokratischen Katechismus' together with two songs, and had told Perrhaivos to re-copy the 'Catechism' and to have all these items printed together with the 'Marshal Khevenhüller', as he called the *Military Manual*.[10] In his old age Perrhaivos spoke of 'a military poem called a Manual' and 'a few provisional political directions'.[11] His memory of it was clearly vague. In any case, it was never distributed, all copies being seized by the Austrian police.

Rhigas admitted that the adaptation of Khevenhüller was his own work; and the Austrian authorities did not believe that he merely copied the 'Catechism'. But the identification of the two songs remained a matter of disagreement until well over a century and a half after his death, because it was mistakenly supposed that they were verbal adaptations of their French and German originals. In reality, as has now been established, they were imitations only of the rhythms of the originals, so that they could be sung to the same tunes.[12] Their opening words, translated into the same metres, would be: 'All of the nations go to war . . . ' (imitating but not translating the 'Carmagnole'); and 'Why thus endure, O friends and brothers all . . . ?' (imitating but not translating 'Freut euch des Lebens'). Rhigas's denial that he had written them did not convince his interrogators.

It is hard to understand why there should ever have been doubt about the identification of the two poems, for the evidence is clear. The first of the two is ascribed to Rhigas by Perrhaivos. He called it the 'second *Thourios*', and included as much as he could remember of it in his *Short Biography*.[13] The full text was found much later in a booklet at Corfu (printed probably in 1798, by Perrhaivos himself), together with a Hymn in praise of Napoleon, which was expressly declared in its title to be set to the tune of the 'Carmagnole'.[14] Since the two poems in the booklet are in identical metre, one or other must have been the 'imitation of the Carmagnole' recorded in the Austrian archives; and since the Hymn in praise of Napoleon refers to his capture of Malta (which took place only days before Rhigas's death) the poem included in the Manual imitating the 'Carmagnole' must be that described by Perrhaivos as the 'second *Thourios*'.

Equally certain is the identification of the song imitating 'Freut euch des Lebens'. It is clear from a passage in a book by the English traveller Henry Holland (later Lord Holland) published in 1812–13, which reads: 'One Romaic song, composed by the unfortunate Rega . . . was sung to the well-known air which we connected with the words of "Life let us cherish" etc.' He goes on to add the Greek words translated as 'Why thus endure . . . ?'[15] There is no need to look further for the original poem; but the supposition of Rhigas's authorship is very dubious, since Perrhaivos claims that he himself wrote the words.

There need be no doubt, however, about Rhigas's authorship of the song imitating the 'Carmagnole', or 'second *Thourios*'. It has features characteristic of his style, such as the invocation of Alexander and other classical heroes. Significant also is the full title, which reads: 'Patriotic Hymn of Hellas and all Greece for the Recovery of their Liberty.' The differentiation between Hellas and Greece (Graikia) is similar to that implied both on the *Map of Hellas* (of which Greece forms only a part) and in the original *Thourios*. Since Perrhaivos states that only the two *Thourioi* were Rhigas's work (for which he has the support of the historian Philemon), there is no good reason to question his claim to have composed the imitation of 'Freut euch des Lebens' himself.[16] The suggestion that Perrhaivos also wrote the 'second *Thourios*' seems absurd; but he may have written the Hymn to Napoleon, which cannot (by reason of its date) have been Rhigas's work.[17]

One work missing from the list of Rhigas's probable compositions is the celebrated 'Greek Marseillaise', sometimes also known as the Paean or National Anthem. This begins with the words which Byron translated in 1811 as 'Sons of the Greeks, arise!' It was never mentioned by Perrhaivos, but it was commonly ascribed to Rhigas in the nineteenth century. Byron and Hobhouse heard it recited, as Rhigas's work, by Andreas Londos at Vostitsa (Aigion) in 1810, 'with a thousand passionate exclamations, the tears streaming down his cheeks'.[18] It was mentioned by Colonel Leake as Rhigas's work in 1814,[19] and often sung as such by the Greek rebels of 1821.[20] As late as 1890, before the Austrian archives on Rhigas's interrogation had been published, it was even identified as the *Thourios* itself.[21]

Even the publication of the Austrian archives did not finally clarify the matter, because they showed some of Rhigas's associates admitting that they had sung the 'Marseillaise' without specifying whether they meant the French original or a Greek adaptation.[22] One of them admitted that he had undertaken to translate the 'Marseillaise', but in fact he only copied it out.[23] This was clearly the French original, but the other cases can only be left in doubt. Modern opinion among Greek scholars is that the 'Greek Marseillaise' or Paean was probably just a popular song at the turn of the century, but not by Rhigas.[24] The canon of poems attributed to him is certainly full of spurious items.[25]

There is in any case enough material in the two reconstructed pamphlets to illustrate the vision by which Rhigas was inspired in the second half of 1797. The moral and cultural emancipation of the Greeks would have to wait; the hour of action was at hand. He envisaged action in three stages, all implied if not explicitly defined in the *New Political Order* and the *Military Manual*. The first stage was an anti-Ottoman conspiracy; the second, a revolutionary war; the third, a democratic restoration of independence.

This was the logical order of proceeding, but Rhigas's vision, and therefore his poet's pen, did not follow such a logical course. Circumstances as well as his temperament precluded it. In the tense, enthusiastic atmosphere of 1797, with the French approaching the Adriatic, it was much easier to envisage the ultimate achievement of his aim than to work out the steps needed to achieve it. When the day of decision came, therefore, he was more prepared both in his mind and on paper for the third stage than for the second, and more prepared for the second than for the first. For the third stage he had the *New Political Order* already in print, and partly in circulation; for the second stage, the *Military Manual* had only just gone to press; but for the first stage his state of readiness was at best extremely doubtful.

He was clearly carried away by unrealistic enthusiasm when he chose to assume that his *New Political Order* would be operative by 1 May 1798, as Article 20 of his Constitution prescribed.[26] Scarcely less unrealistic, although the *Military Manual* was in the press, was the choice of Marshal Khevenhüller's Concise Theory as a basis for the second stage. Khevenhüller's doctrines were designed for a well-drilled, well-equipped modern army. If Napoleon were to make French troops available for the liberation of Greece, he had no need of any instruction from an Austrian Field-Marshal who had been dead for more than half a century. If not, as was to be the case, there were neither the time nor the means to apply Khevenhüller's doctrines to the guerrillas of Souli, Roumeli and the Mani on whom Rhigas would have to rely.

It was only for the third and last stage of his mission that Rhigas's material was completely ready. Three thousand copies of the *New Political Order* were printed in November, or possibly in some cases earlier, for a few copies were said to have been in the hands of his associates in October.[27] Of the contents, only the opening 'Proclamation' and the *Thourios* were entirely original works of Rhigas's pen. Both the 'Rights of Man' and the 'Constitution' were modelled on the French originals; but they contained innovations adapting them, as Rhigas put it, to 'the Greek spirit'.[28]

The 'Proclamation' is a kind of prose summary of the *Thourios*, equally vigorous and eloquent.[29] It begins with an address to 'the people descended from the Hellenes', together with all the victims of Ottoman tyranny, 'both Christians and Turks, without any distinction of religion (since all are creatures of God and children of the first-created)'. It laments that 'the most beautiful kingdom in the world, extolled by wise men everywhere, has fallen into a terrible anarchy, so that no one, of whatever class or religion, can be sure either of his life or of his honour or of his possessions'. It declares that the people has therefore decided to rebel, to overthrow this tyranny, and to embrace freedom.

It is noteworthy that apart from the opening phrase, there is no further mention of Hellenes or Greeks. All the peoples of 'Roumeli, Asia Minor, the Mediterranean islands and Vlachobogdania' are addressed. Each is urged 'to hold up before his eyes as it were a bright mirror, the foundations of freedom, of security, and

of his happiness'. It concludes that 'the following public proclamation of the precious Rights of Man and of the free inhabitants
of this kingdom is gloriously decreed'. There follow the 35 articles of the 'Rights of Man', 124 of the 'Constitution', and an
Appendix on the flag and the armed forces of the Hellenic
Republic (which is still called from time to time 'this kingdom').

In both the 'Rights of Man' and the 'Constitution' itself, Rhigas closely followed the number and order of the articles in his
French models. Four French Constitutions (1789, 1791, 1793,
and 1795) were introduced during his lifetime, none of which
had time to take practical effect. To each was prefixed a Declaration of the Rights of Man, but the versions varied. Rhigas used as
his chief model the Constitution of 1793, with its accompanying
Declaration. He introduced a few amendments from the Constitution of 1795 when he belatedly became aware of it, and many
explanatory glosses of his own 'in the Greek spirit'. He made
even more extensive amendments on his own initiative to the
'Rights of Man'.

At the beginning of the *New Political Order* he prefixed a qua-
train from his own *Thourios* (lines 23–6):

Let us place enlightened councillors and patriots
To have all things under their command.
Let Law be the first and only guide,
And let there be one leader of the fatherland.

The word 'leader' should not be misunderstood, any more than
the word 'kingdom'. Rhigas was introducing a 'new political
order', but he could not help using current terminology. Neither
word is inconsistent with his intention to establish a democratic
republic. He was borrowing from the French a prescription formulated after the revolution had taken place and succeeded, in
order to transfer it to a country where the revolution was still to
come. Even so, a Greek constitutional lawyer has judged Rhigas's
'Constitution' to be 'more liberal, more democratic, and more
humane' than its French archetype.[30]

His first significant but inconspicuous amendment is in the title
of the 'Rights of Man'.[31] The French Declaration spoke of the
'Rights of Man and Citizen'. Rhigas drops the restrictive word

'Citizen', thus enlarging the scope of the Declaration. Being a homogeneous nation, the French did not need to look beyond their own citizens. Rhigas was looking to dozens of different nationalities, and even to all humanity. For the same reason he adds the words 'Christians and Turks' to the French formula: 'All men are equal by natural reason' (art. 3).* Later, in quoting the French Declaration that any injury to one citizen was an injury to all, he adds the words: 'The Bulgar must bestir himself when the Greek suffers, and *vice versa*; and both for the Albanian and the Vlach' (art. 34).

In the following passages, the words in inverted commas are additions by Rhigas to the French text. The law is identical 'regardless of class or wealth, for the same offences' (art. 3). The rulers have a duty not to exercise oppression, and 'if they govern badly, they must be dismissed' (art. 9). Cruel treatment, 'such as chains, insults or beating', is forbidden before conviction (art. 13). Legislation may not be retrospective, but in the case of theft, although it cannot be punished retrospectively, 'the thief must return what he stole' (art. 14). An employer 'may not insult or beat his employee' (art. 18). Rhigas did not, of course, imply that the French took a different view of these principles. The difference was that he was legislating for people who might not take them for granted after centuries of foreign despotism.

There are, however, some striking deviations of principle from the French text. The French draftsmen in 1793, in the midst of the Terror, prescribed the death penalty for anyone who tried to 'usurp the sovereignty' of the nation; Rhigas more mildly prescribes that he should be 'imprisoned by the free people, tried and punished according to the law' (art. 27). In effect, the death penalty was to be abolished. An equally liberal-minded innovation is Rhigas's provision for the universal education of both boys and girls (art. 22). 'From letters is born the progress with which all free peoples shine', he added. He prescribes that French and Italian must be taught at schools in the towns, and the classical historians must be translated (presumably into demotic Greek). These provisions are more explicit than the corresponding article

* Citations from the 'Rights of Man' are printed in lower case (art. 1, etc.); those from the 'Constitution' in upper case (Art.1, etc.). The numbers are identical with the French originals.

in the French Declaration, which did not prescribe (though perhaps it assumed) equality of the sexes in education.

It has been inconclusively debated whether Rhigas intended that equality of education should also confer on women political equality. Since he provides in the Constitution (Art. 109 and Appendix) that women as well as men should be liable for military service, the right to vote would logically seem to follow. But in the haste with which Rhigas compiled his revolutionary texts, and especially his explanatory additions to the French texts, he failed to deal with the point explicitly. If he could have been asked, he would probably have replied affirmatively.

Hasty draftsmanship comes out again in his version of the right to rebel against tyranny (art. 35). Once more, he was thinking in anticipation of a liberal revolution, whereas the French revolution had already succeeded when its principles were put into writing. So the right of rebellion in Rhigas's version is elaborated in a long paragraph to which the French version has no parallel. In naïvely enthusiastic phrases, he describes how 'the bravest and most freedom-loving patriots must seize the cross-roads and mountain heights until their numbers grow'. He prescribes the details of their organisation in units of ascending size, under officers of specified rank, up to 'a commander-in-chief over a number of generals'.

These are clearly, in reality, instructions for the initial rising against Ottoman tyranny rather than against a hypothetical tyranny after liberation. In the same paragraph, which reflects his impetuosity as well as the urgency of his task, Rhigas concludes with a quite unrelated provision for the cancellation of public and private debts of more than five years standing, provided that interest has been paid (presumably at 20per cent *per annum*). This was an afterthought which he owed to a classical reminiscence of Solon rather than to any French source.

Like the 'Rights of Man', Rhigas's 'Constitution' also shows signs of haste in its composition.[32] As late as June 1797, he had not yet seen the French text. He wrote to Antonios Koronios at Trieste in that month asking him to send either a copy or a translation of it.[33] Koronios delayed sending it, perhaps in fear of the anti-Jacobinism which was then rampant in Vienna. Rhigas, however, obtained a copy of the 1793 Constitution from Bucharest, either through George Poulios or from the French Consulate. He was still unaware that it had been superseded by the 1795 Constitution. In response to a further letter, Koronios eventually sent him what he called 'nine chapters' of the Constitution which he had obtained from a ship's captain calling at Trieste from Venice.[34] Rhigas replied that this did not correspond with the version which he had received from Bucharest. Clearly the 'nine chapters' were from the 1795 Constitution, which was then nominally in force. This point was missed by the Austrian interrogators who questioned Rhigas and Koronios in 1798.

Nine 'chapters' could have amounted to some 300 Articles of the 1795 Constitution; but as Koronios also said that he had sent only a 'small part' of the whole, he probably meant nine Articles only. Being fearful of the consequences, Koronios also claimed to have made his translation 'unintelligible', which would explain the very limited use that Rhigas made of it. In fact, he adopted only two Articles from the 1795 Constitution, not without causing some confusion in the process of combining them with the 1793 version.

In one case, he followed the French example by setting up two legislative bodies (as in 1795) instead of one (as in 1793). This caused no drafting problem (Art. 39). But in the other case, he followed the French in reducing the size of the Directory from 24 to five. This in itself caused no drafting problem (Art. 62). He failed, however, to amend his Article 64, which followed the French Constitution of 1793 in providing that 'half the members of the Directory retire each year'. This provision clearly could not be carried out under his revised Article 62.[35]

The inconsistency would easily have been resolved if Rhigas had had time; but he had not. Koronios's extracts from the French Constitution of 1795 reached him only at the end of July. By then events were moving very fast. The French had already occupied Venice and overthown the Republic of the Doges. They were also in occupation of the Ionian Islands, and Napoleon's representatives were enjoying a warm welcome from Ali Pasha in Ioannina.[36] Rhigas knew what was going on from correspondents in many parts of Greece. On 5 August he wrote to Koronios that they were pressing him for action.[37] The pressure was transmitted by way of Bucharest, but its sources were Greeks who had connections in Thessaly, Epiros, and even Athens. He would have to finish his work quickly if he were to offer the French an acceptable basis for co-operation.

He gained time by following the French model even more closely in the 'Constitution' than in the 'Rights of Man', with very few modifications: perhaps too closely, and too few, considering that the French Constitution was designed for a unitary, homogeneous state, whereas his own was for a multi-national state with different languages, different religions, and different histories. His main amendments were addressed to this very point: that despite the diversity of its constituents, the Hellenic Republic was to be a unitary state. That unity is expressly affirmed in Articles 1, 2 and 7.

These early articles establish an inescapable fact: that the 'Greek spirit' must be predominant over all the races comprised in the Hellenic Republic. The ambiguity of the term 'Hellenes' is more obvious today than it was in Rhigas's time. It stood both for the people of the proposed Republic as a whole and for the Greek-speaking Orthodox component on its own. No alternative term for the latter is used in the 'Constitution'. The ambiguity is unmistakable in the definition of the 'Hellenic Republic', one and indivisible (Art. 1), as comprising 'Hellenes, Bulgars, Albanians, Vlachs, Armenians, Turks, and any other kind of race' (Art. 7).

Rhigas's 'Constitution' never escaped from this linguistic ambiguity, which must have caused trouble if it had ever been put into effect. There was nothing in the French Constitutions to help him; nor did he ever consider a federal system on the American model. The English-speaking world was quite alien to him: there is no evidence, for example, that he ever studied Thomas Paine's version of the 'Rights of Man', which had been published in 1791–92. French examples alone interested him, but they did not answer all his problems, because the French did not have to deal with racial minorities.

Rhigas's Articles on citizenship are necessarily more complex than his French models. He begins by adopting the exact phraseology of the French version (Art. 4). But what follows shows, by implication, that it would be much easier for a Greek-speaker, a

Christian (even if not a Greek-speaker) or a well-qualified westerner to acquire citizenship than it would for a Muslim, a Turk, or any other foreigner. The predominance in southeast Europe of the Greek language, the Orthodox Patriarchate, the education and culture of the Greeks, made this element of chauvinism not merely inevitable but virtually unconscious.

Besides the normal criteria copied from the French text, citizenship is also to be conferred on anyone who speaks the demotic or Hellenic (classical) language, and is a benefactor of the country, 'even if he lives in the Antipodes, for the Hellenic leaven is spread over the two hemispheres'. It will be conferred, too, on anyone who is a Christian not speaking demotic or classical Greek, 'suffice it that he be a benefactor of Hellas'; and also on any foreigner who is judged worthy by the government: for example, an artist, teacher, or deserving patriot. The highest honour is for a foreign philosopher or European artist who settles in Greece to teach. He is not merely to become a citizen but to have a statue put up to him, and his life is to be recorded by an outstanding Greek writer.[38]

In this long and largely original Article, Rhigas has evidently not thought out fully the consequences of his additions to his French model. His thoughts were running faster than his pen. In the immediately following Article, his haste shows itself in another way. He adopts and elaborates the three grounds provided in the French text for deprivation of citizenship (Art. 5). He then adds an eloquent but irrelevant paragraph in praise of the good citizen, who acquires skilled experience and knowledge abroad and then returns to give his country the benefit of them. It is hardly necessary even to imply that such a citizen will not be deprived of his citizenship.

In more than a hundred remaining articles, Rhigas scarcely departs from the French text. Where he does so, his amendments are always in the direction of more explicit democracy. In Article 21, for example, the French text states that the nation is represented by the totality of the population; Rhigas adds: 'not merely by the rich and prominent'. In Article 60, the French text provides that if objection is taken to any law, the legislative body will convoke the primary (local) assemblies; Rhigas expands this to provide for a kind of popular referendum:

If ten per cent of the primary assemblies in each province dissents, then the Legislative Assembly will convene the primary assemblies and the whole people will be asked to express its opinion.

A further gloss on the definition of popular sovereignty guarantees the rights of citizenship to 'Hellenes, Turks, Armenians, Jews, and every nationality to be found settled in the Republic' (Art. 122). The addition of the Jews rests on a manuscript found at Bucharest only in 1962, but there is no reason to suppose that Rhigas omitted them in his original draft.[39] On the other hand, the omission of most of the Balkan peoples by name suggests that in this instance Rhigas comprised them all under the term 'Hellenes'.

Here again the problems of a multi-national population had not affected the French draftsmen. But Rhigas saw that it was impossible to make all the languages of his Hellenic Republic equally official, so he settled on the *lingua franca* of south-east Europe, which was Greek; but it was to be demotic Greek, not classical. All decrees and laws, and all public documents, must be written 'in the simple language of the Hellenes' (Art. 53). This provision, which he was the first to formulate, had to wait 180 years before it was put into effect.

A still more far-reaching innovation was the extension of military service to include women. Rhigas added to the French provision for universal military service that 'even women must carry javelins if they cannot handle a firearm' (Art. 109). This provision, together with that for educational equality, justifies the assumption that Rhigas would have extended the franchise to women. The conscription of women is also confirmed in the Appendix to the 'Constitution', which has no analogue in the French original; though a remarkable report in the *Ephimeris* of 12 March 1792 shows the women of Paris demanding the right to military service for themselves.[40]

The final 'Appendix' is primarily concerned with military insignia. The flag is to depict Herakles' club with three crosses above it (like Rhigas's own lost seal). The colours, in three horizontal bands, are to be: black, to signify a soldier's death for freedom and his country; white, to signify the purity of 'our just cause'; and red, to signify the imperial purple and sovereignty. Rhigas adds that red was worn in the past to disguise the blood from wounds, 'so that soldiers may not be afraid'. He might also have added that the purple represented the heritage of the Byzantine Emperors.

Besides the flag, he also defines the uniform and equipment of the army. Every soldier is to wear a helmet and the 'heroic dress', consisting of a black tunic, a white shirt, and red boots or stockings. Women as well as men—indeed, 'every inhabitant of the Republic', since all are liable to military service—must wear on their helmets a club of Herakles, painted or embroidered on white cloth, or perhaps on tin. 'This is the sign by which free democrats and equal brothers may recognise each other.'

That is the end of the 'Appendix', and with it of the 'Constitution'. But one point of military organisation not found in Rhigas's French model can be added from his 'Rights of Man'. He specifies there the ranks which are to come into effect in wartime (art. 35), though at peace 'all are equal and brothers' (Art. 111). The ranks are as follows, in ascending order: a decemvir, commanding 10 men; a sub-centurion, commanding 50; a centurion, commanding 100; a chiliarch, commanding 10 centurions; a general, commanding three chiliarchs; and a commander-in-chief, commanding an unspecified number of generals.

A particular interest of the proposed system lies in the fact that Nicholas Ypsilantis, the grandson of Rhigas's first patron and son of his former fellow-student, laid down exactly the same ranks in the regulations which he drew up for the Greek revolution of 1821; and he also prescribed the same flag as Rhigas, giving the same interpretation of the colours.[41] Undoubtedly he must have been one of those who somehow came to see a copy of Rhigas's *New Political Order*.

The final item in Rhigas's revolutionary compilation was the *Thourios*.[42] It was already well known among the Greeks; it had been circulated in manuscript, and sung many times. Greeks have always recognised it as Rhigas's masterpiece, combining noble rhetoric with enlightened vision. One couplet is on every Greek's lips:

Better one hour of life in freedom
Than forty years of bondage and prison!   (7–8)

If the story is true of his last night on Mount Olympus before he
left Greece for ever, this couplet was the first he ever composed.[43]

He prepared the way for it in the finished version with six lines
almost betraying despair:

How long, my heroes, shall we live in bondage,
Alone like lions on ridges, on peaks?
Living in caves, gazing on the scrub-land,
Turning from the world to bitter enslavement?
Losing our brothers, our country, our fathers,
Our friends, our children, and all our kin?   (1–6)

A total of 63 couplets ends with a summary of Rhigas's appeal for
action:

Let us slay the wolves who impose the yoke,
Who cruelly oppress both Christians and Turks;
Let the Cross shine over land and sea;
Let the foe kneel down in the face of justice;
Let men be purged of all this sickness;
And let us live on earth, as brothers, free!   (121–6)

The last three couplets are revealing as well as eloquent: they
expose Rhigas's life-long dilemma. He wanted to be non-discrim-
inating between Muslims and Christians, Turks and Greeks, and
also between Greeks and their fellow-Christians. But he could
not ignore the fact that the Greeks, as the more highly developed
and educated, were bound to predominate in his Hellenic
Republic, both over the Turks and other Muslims and over the
other Christians. Thus, on the one hand, he lays down the same
rule as in his 'Constitution':

Let everyone live freely in his faith;   (43)

but on the other hand he repeatedly asserts the supremacy of the
Cross:

Let us make the oath upon the Cross!   (22)
High on our standards raise up the Cross!   (109)

Again, in a spirit of fairness, he juxtaposes in consecutive lines an exaltation of the Cross and a denunciation of those who oppress Turks as well (lines 121–2).

He never resolved this dilemma; he only veiled it in the torrent of his verse. Between the first three couplets and the last three, he invokes by name not only all the races of the Ottoman Empire but many of their individual leaders; and he does not hesitate to criticise by name Christians as well as Muslims whom he finds slow to respond. In the upshot, it may be said that the ethnography and prosopography of the *Thourios* correspond closely with the cartography of his *Map of Hellas*, at any rate as it would have appeared if all 24 sheets had been completed. It was under the name of Hellas that he hoped all racial and religious differences would be reconciled. It is Hellas in the *Thourios* that calls upon both Muslims and Christians to rebel (lines 83–4). But it is hard to believe that the name would have been a sufficient solvent of historic feuds.

The *Thourios*, however, is not to be regarded as a blueprint: it was a fanfare. Its historical value lies in its identification, by name or implication, of the forces which Rhigas was trying to recruit to his revolution. Some are castigated for cowardice or for collaboration with the Ottoman power; all are called on to rebel. The first to be named are Phanariotes and members of other prominent families. But there are some indications that his list is obsolete, and the lines (11–16) might have been composed at an earlier date.

He addresses anonymously a Vizier, a Dragoman and a Lord; of whom the first must be a Turk, the second a Greek, and the third might be either. Next, he names half a dozen prominent Greeks to be regarded as a 'mirror' or model. They include a Soutzos (presumably Rhigas's own employer), and also a Mourouzis, a Ghikas and a Mavroyenis. Alexander Mourouzis had been Hospodar of Vallachia from 1793 to 1796, but no Ghika had held office in the Danubian principalities since 1777, and Nicholas Mavroyenis had been executed in 1790. A relative of the last, Ioannis Mavroyenis, was living in Vienna and was well known to Rhigas, but it is inconceivable that he can have been meant since no one would have responded to his leadership.

The *Thourios* goes on to address whole classes who had resisted Ottoman tyranny and suffered for doing so: 'brave captains, priests, men of the people', and also agas—again the subject Turks as well as the Greeks (lines 17–18). The one Muslim leader addressed by name is Pasvanoglou (line 87), but it is implied that he is dilatory. Others who are identified only by their places of office are the pashas of Brusa, Georgia and Aleppo, the beys of Egypt, and provincial governors in the Ukraine (as it now is) and the Danubian principalities (lines 91–104). Rhigas calls for the flame of revolution to spread from Bosnia to Arabia.

All of them are to be united by an oath, which is set out in five couplets (lines 33–42). It is addressed to the 'King of the Universe', who could be regarded as impartial with respect to the different faiths, though the oath is also to be sworn on the Cross (lines 21–2). The rebels are to declare a determination to destroy the existing tyranny and a loyal obedience to the 'General', who is unnamed and undefined. The oath ends:

And if I break the oath, may Heaven hurl lightning
And burn me to a cinder, that I turn to smoke!   (41–2)

There is no evidence that anyone ever formally swore an oath in these words; nor was the oath even secret, since the whole *Thourios* was well known. It can be regarded simply as a passionate aspiration. But Rhigas's close associates, who often sang the *Thourios*, must have regarded that very act as constituting an oath. This necessarily has a bearing on the much-discussed question: was there an organised conspiracy, and did Rhigas in fact found what the Greeks call a *hetairia* or secret society?

❂   ❂   ❂

[1] Vranousis (1953), 62; Amantos (1930), 84–5.
[2] Legrand, 64–5.
[3] Amantos (1930), 162–5; Legrand 66–7.
[4] Daskalakis (1937), 24.
[5] Amantos (1930), 44–83; Daskalakis (1962), 14–16.
[6] Amantos (1930), 20–1.
[7] Full texts, with French predecessors, in Daskalakis (1962), 74-111; text in Greek alone in Papageorgiou, 5–38;
English translation in Clogg (1976), 149–63.
[8] Daskalakis (1937), 36–8.
[9] Enepekidis (1955/a) 165, 388–96; Amantos (1930), 165.
[10] Legrand, 66-7.
[11] Perrhaivos (1860), 19.
[12] Vranousis (1960), 5–39; Pistas (1969), 194–204.
[13] Perrhaivos (1860), 12; full text in Papageorgiou, 41-8; also Vranousis (1953), 394–7; Daskalakis (1964), 436–40.

[14] Vranousis (1953), 17–21.
[15] Holland, 322–3.
[16] Perrhaivos (1860), 12–18; 35–7; Philemon (1834), 98–9, n. (a).
[17] Lambros (1905), 651–2.
[18] Hobhouse, II. 586.
[19] Leake, I. 157.
[20] Gordon, I. 40; Amantos (1930), xxiii, n. 2.
[21] Lambros (1916), 72.
[22] Amantos (1930), 160–1; Legrand 82–3.
[23] Amantos (1930), 166–7.
[24] Daskalakis (1937), 45–52.
[25] *Ibid.*, 53–7.
[26] Daskalakis (1962), 91.
[27] Legrand, 102–3.
[28] *Ibid.*, 68–9.
[29] Daskalakis (1962), 74–6; Vranousis (1953), 371; Papageorgiou, 10–11.
[30] Svolos, 738.
[31] Daskalakis (1962), 76–86; Vranousis (1953), 372-6; Papageorgiou, 12–18.
[32] Daskalakis (1962), 86–111; Vranousis (1953), 377–88; Papageorgiou, 19–38.
[33] Legrand, 68–71.
[34] *Ibid.*, 96–9.
[35] Daskalakis (1962), 38–41.
[36] Bonaparte, VI. 72.
[37] Legrand, 72–3.
[38] Daskalakis (1962), 87–8.
[39] *Ibid.*, 136.
[40] Laios (1961), 57.
[41] Daskalakis (1962), 121–2, 138; Philemon (1859), I. 69.
[42] Text, with French translation, in Fauriel, II. 20-9. Original text, as printed in Corfu (1798), in Lambros (1916), 73–4; also in Vranousis (1953), 390–3. A modern French translation is in Botzaris, 205–9; an incomplete English version in Dalven, 65–7.
[43] N. G. Politis, 15.

VI

A VISION OF CONSPIRACY

NICHOLAS Ypsilantis and Christopher Perrhaivos both distinguished between the 'first *hetairia*', which was that of Rhigas, and the 'second *hetairia*', which was the *Philiki Hetairia* of the revolution in 1821.[1] But they differed in their accounts of the first. For Ypsilantis, it was a benevolent society of blood brotherhood and mutual support including Turks as well as Greeks; this could hardly have been secret, let alone a conspiracy. For Perrhaivos, it was a revolutionary conspiracy confined to Greeks. The two accounts can only be reconciled by assuming that Rhigas's earlier benevolent society was later replaced by, or transformed into, Perrhaivos's secret conspiracy. The question has been complicated by the universal awareness that the *Philiki Hetairia* was undeniably a conspiracy; its mere name has cast a retrospective colouring on Rhigas's movement.

There is no compelling reason for these *hetairiai* to be regarded as two of a kind. There could be, and were, all sorts of benevolent societies among expatriate Greeks, of a social or cultural character, both before and after Rhigas. There were masonic lodges and merchants' guilds. There were clubs of either nationalist or Jacobin inspiration throughout south-east Europe, including a Society of Friends at Bucharest (1780), a Popular Club at Constantinople (1794), and clubs with French affiliations in the Ionian Islands even before the arrival of Napoleon's General Gentili in 1797. All were regarded as conspiracies by the police.

But a conspiratorial society must have distinctive characteristics: at least a clandestine charter and membership, a system of initiation, a secret oath of loyalty, a cellular organisation, and the use of code-names and ciphers. A quarter of a century later, the *Philiki Hetairia* had all of them. It has yet to be shown that Rhigas's movement had the like, unless the oath embodied in the *Thourios* is to be regarded as evidence.

Perrhaivos was emphatic, however, that Rhigas did found a *hetairia* comparable to the 'second *hetairia*', and that he himself was a member of both. He did so not only in his biography of

Rhigas, published in his old age (1860), but in his earlier *War Memoirs* (1836), much closer to the events;[2] and he referred to Rhigas's *hetairia* in his still earlier correspondence with Andreas Idromenos, a priest and schoolmaster on Corfu, between 1797 and 1818, before the *Philiki Hetairia* had become a real force.[3] The assumption that Rhigas was the central figure in such a *hetairia* is also to be found in the records of the Austrian interrogators in 1798, which refer more than once to such a *Gesellschaft*.[4]

Even in his old age, Perrhaivos was careful to distinguish between those who were members of the *hetairia* and those who were not. He identifies very few members by name: Antonios Koronios at Trieste;[5] a Dr Kyritzis at Ioannina;[6] and of course himself, expressly described as a 'conspirator' as well (*synomotis*, implying an oath).[7] He also speaks, without naming names, of various 'large-scale merchants' in Vienna, from families originating in Epiros, Thessaly and Macedonia, who were compromised;[8] and of 'the most intelligent and practical members' in Vienna, whom Rhigas used to convene two or three times a week for discussion.[9] Of all these, Koronios was the only one named who was executed with Rhigas. How widespread then was the *hetairia* as Perrhaivos understood the term? Did it even, in a formal sense, exist at all as an organised conspiracy?

These questions are best addressed by examining first the list of those arrested by the Austrian police, and then the somewhat vaguer list of those who also came under suspicion. Sixteen men, including Rhigas, were eventually arrested and interrogated.[10] They were divided into two groups, not by their degree of guilt but by their national status. Ten, including Rhigas, were Ottoman subjects by birth. The other six were Austrian subjects, except for one who had Russian nationality. The first group were liable to extradition, though there was no formal treaty of extradition with the Ottoman government.

The following belonged, with Rhigas, to the first group:[11] Evstratios (or Evstathios) Argentis, a merchant from Chios, aged 31; Antonios Koronios, also a merchant from Chios, aged 27; Dimitrios Nikolidis, a medical teacher from Zitsa in Epiros, aged 32; Ioannis Emmanuel, a medical student from Kastoria in Macedonia, aged 24; his brother Panayotis, a book-keeper in Argentis's employment, aged 22; Theocharis Torountzias, a merchant from

Macedonia, aged 22; Ioannis Karatzas, a churchwarden from Nicosia in Cyprus, aged 31; Andreas Masoutis[12] from Larisa in Thessaly, formerly employed by Argentis, aged 35; and Constantine Amoiros from Chios, a clerk employed by Argentis, aged 38. The last two were not regarded by the Austrian police as conspirators, and were released after a short time.

The following were the six non-Ottoman subjects:[13] Philippos Petrovits, a clerk to Argentis, born in Croatia, aged 18; George Theocharis, a commercial agent from Kastoria, aged 40; George Poulios, described as a journalist (in fact, an editor, printer and publisher), from Siatista in Macedonia, aged 32; Kaspar Peters, a teacher of French, born in Westphalia, aged 40; Constantine Toullios, the son of a merchant at Pest, aged 18; and Constantine Doukas,[14] a Russian subject from Siatista, aged 45. All were of Greek descent (Petrovits through his mother), except Peters, who was a native-born Austrian.

All of those named were resident in the Austrian Empire, but the authorities believed that the conspiracy went much wider. About a hundred names appear in the Austrian records, of Rhigas's associates or associates of his associates. Some twenty of them were resident in the Danubian principalities; the rest were more or less equally divided between the Austrian and Ottoman territories. Few names on the Greek mainland became known to the Austrian authorities, but most of those resident in the Austrian Empire had either been born in Greece or had roots there no more than a generation back.

Although those arrested and interrogated formed, for the Austrian authorities, the core of the conspiracy, there is a significant number of absentees from the list, for various reasons. A striking example is Perrhaivos himself, a self-confessed conspirator who was with Rhigas when he was arrested. Perrhaivos claimed, quite falsely, to be a French citizen, and was accepted as such by the French Consul at Trieste;[15] but it is remarkable that the Austrian police did not override this bogus protection.

Several other Greeks, who were at Trieste when Rhigas was arrested there, were hardly less compromised than Perrhaivos. Two of them—Antonios Niotis and George Kalaphatis—were the addressees of a number of boxes containing propaganda material which Rhigas had sent in advance from Vienna.[16] The

Austrians correctly identified Niotis from his initials on three boxes,[17] but apparently failed to identify Kalaphatis from the initials G. C. on two others. They might both have been already under suspicion if the police had been sufficiently alert. In the summer of 1797, Rhigas had sent to Niotis 600 sets of the *Map of Hellas* to be forwarded to Smyrna for distribution.[18] In the same summer, Kalaphatis had been present when Koronios read out Rhigas's *Thourios* to a small audience at Trieste which also included Dimitrios Oikonomos, the man who betrayed Rhigas; and all except Oikonomos had been deeply moved by the poem.[19] These facts came out in interrogation, but the police never attempted to lay hands on Niotis or Kalaphatis.

Other Greeks at Trieste were liable to suspicion, simply because it was there that Rhigas was arrested; but none of them was molested by the police. Oikonomos, who was Koronios's partner in business, was naturally exempt as Rhigas's betrayer. So was his brother, another partner in his business. Another merchant, Nicholas Plastaras, who had urged Oikonomos to keep quiet about Rhigas's activities, was also left free. So were others to whom Argentis gave Rhigas letters of introduction;[20] and others again who were known to have been present when Koronios read out Rhigas's *Thourios* at Trieste.[21]

Perhaps the most suspect character at Trieste who escaped investigation was Michael Tournavitis, a brother of Dimitraki, who had been Rhigas's colleague as secretary to Michael Soutzos at Bucharest. Rathkeal, the Austrian Ambassador at Constantinople, had suggested that an examination of the correspondence between the two brothers would be revealing.[22] If this had been done, it would probably have led to suspicion of Michael Tournavitis's links with Nicholas Plastaras and Paraskhos Katsaros, for all three had contributed financially to the privateering fleet formed by Lambros Katsonis at Trieste in 1790, to harass the Turks.[23] Moreover, the Austrians knew from Nikolidis's interrogation that Katsaros had at least once been guilty of singing the 'Marseillaise'.[24] Yet they did not pursue Rathkeal's suggestion of investigating Tournavitis's associates.

The neighbouring port of Venice was also full of Greeks who might have come under suspicion, most of them originating in the Ionian Islands. Venice was occupied by the French in May

1797; so was Corfu a month later. But in October Venice passed under Austrian jurisdiction by the Treaty of Campo Formio. The Austrian authorities were convinced that Venice was a centre of Greek conspiracy, which was natural enough in view of the ease of communication with both Trieste and Corfu.[25] It was from Venice, for example, that Koronios received a copy of the French Constitution to pass on to Rhigas; and by the same route that the proclamation to the Corfiotes by Napoleon's General Gentili reached Trieste.[26] But there is no case on record of any Greek arrested by the Austrians at Venice, although several, including the poet Ioannis Vilaras, were under suspicion.[27]

In the Ionian Islands there were Greek sympathisers too numerous to be catalogued. They had always enjoyed free and widespread emigration: to Venice, to Austria, to Russia, and many other European countries. Several crossed Rhigas's path in Vienna or Trieste. George Vendotis, from Zakynthos, was closely associated with him in Vienna until his death in 1795.[28] Gabriel Palatinos, from Cephallonia, who had entered the Russian service, was instrumental in helping Perrhaivos to evade arrest.[29] Dionysios Romas, who was Venetian Consul General at Patras, was said to have come to Trieste expressly to meet Rhigas.[30] He was described in a funeral oration, 60 years later, as a member of Rhigas's *hetairia*. But even if he were at Trieste when Rhigas was arrested, he would not have been in danger himself. The Austrians would not have dared to arrest anyone who could claim a connection with the Ionian Islands while these were under French protection.

It was at Vienna, naturally, that Rhigas's associates were in the greatest danger from the police. Yet it is surprising how many were left unmolested in spite of coming under suspicion. The commonest grounds of suspicion were to have attended meetings at which the *Thourios* was read or sung, or to have handled copies of the *New Political Order* (always miscalled the *Proclamation* by the Austrians). Of the six men who are known to have heard the *Thourios* recited for the first time[31] in September 1796, four were arrested; but only one (Argentis) shared Rhigas's fate; three (Masoutis and Amoiros at Vienna, and Polyzos at Yassy) were held only for a short time; and two (Mizanis and Sevastos) were not even arrested, although both were Ottoman subjects and therefore liable to extradition. Such were the vagaries of Austrian justice.

Count von Pergen was nevertheless convinced that many Greeks in Vienna knew of Rhigas's 'revolutionary plans' and that the 'central organisation' was located there.[32] Insofar as there were plans and an organisation at all, he was no doubt right. But it is surprising that his police failed even to arrest men expressly implicated by several witnesses in the course of interrogation: for example, Michael Sterios, who was described by Argentis as 'deeply interested in the liberation of Greece'. He even had copies of the *New Political Order* in his possession, and knew about Rhigas's attempt to establish a correspondence with Napoleon. He told Panayotis Emmanuel on 18 November 1797 that Rhigas was about to go to Greece, where the revolution would begin within three months. All of these suspicious revelations came out during the interrogation of those under arrest.[33] Yet the police never laid a finger on Sterios.

At Pest there were similar contrasts of fortune which were just as surprising. Three of the suspects—Torountzias, Karatzas and Toullios—were arrested there. Unfortunately all three implicated each other over the possession of copies of the *New Political Order*. They also implicated other Greeks at Pest, though not invariably by name. Torountzias admitted that he had met many Greeks in a café there, who knew about the *New Political Order*. He himself had shown copies to friends. The family and employees of a merchant at Pest called Rizos Dormouzis already had a copy. Other Greeks at Pest who were under suspicion, including two medical students, were known by name.[34] Yet there were no other arrests.

Torountzias also had a circle of friends and business partners at Semlin (now Zemun), the last Austrian outpost on the Danube before the Ottoman frontier. His brother George lived there, as did a number of merchants whose names became known to the authorities. Torountzias's complicity with Rhigas was undeniable, and it involved his associates as well. He sent to his brother three sets of the *Map of Hellas* and fifty copies of the 'pictures' (presumably of Alexander the Great); and he admitted knowing Rhigas's purpose in publishing them. During his own visits to Semlin, he and his brother would sing the *Thourios* with a group of merchants, and later they read the *New Political Order*.[35] None of this was denied, but only Torountizas suffered for it. He was

86

handed over to the Turks to be executed, not because he was especially guilty but because he was an Ottoman subject, born in Macedonia; so was Karatzas, because he was born in Cyprus; but Toullios was not, because he was born in the Austrian Empire.

Others who were regarded by the Austrian authorities as members of the conspiracy were removed from the scene by fate or chance or simple evasion. Ioannis Mavroyenis, whose name was implicated by several of Rhigas's associates, though he later tried to deny any connection with Rhigas, was absent in northern Europe. George Poulios's brother Publius was in Vallachia selling books and distributing propaganda. Dr Polyzos was in Moldavia, where he held a teaching post at the Academy of Yassy; although he was arrested there, nothing was proved against him. A number of merchants at Vienna supplied Rhigas with letters to take to Greece, but these were destroyed in the nick of time when he was arrested.

The most vigorous antagonist of Rhigas and the Greeks in general was Rathkeal, the Austrian Ambassador in Constantinople.[36] He was convinced that the conspiracy extended to the Danubian principalities. At Bucharest his chief suspects were Gaudin at the French Consulate, presumably under the influence of his Greek wife, and Tournavitis through his contacts with Gaudin, Rhigas, Pasvanoglou and his own brother at Trieste. Rathkeal was also convinced that forged passports were being issued to Turkish subjects (presumbly Greek conspirators) at Cherson in Russia. He repeatedly pressed his Consul at Yassy to seek information on the subject, particularly from Polyzos while he was under arrest.[37]

It would have been idle for Rhigas to deny that he had contacts in the Danubian principalities, since he had lived there for years. A number of names were extracted by the Austrian authorities from a note-book in his possession, in which they appeared in abbreviated and confused form.[38] Among them it is posssible to identify several friends from earlier days: Emmanuel Brancoveanu, his first employer; Lambros Photiadis, now head of the Academy of Bucharest; and the Romanian scholars and poets, Iordache Slătineanu and Iordache Golescu. None of these could seriously be regarded as conspirators.

The rest of the names, which cannot easily be identified, were probably those of merchants, with whom Rhigas's connections may have been quite innocent; though commercial correspondence could easily have led to, or served as cover for, less innocent communication. It is true that the one letter to Rhigas from Bucharest which is quoted in the Austrian archives, though not preserved in full, was undeniably an incitement to promote an armed rebellion in Greece.[39] But in any case Vallachia and Moldavia were beyond Austrian jurisdiction. So were a range of other places where Rhigas's note-book named contacts—Preveza, Patras, Ioannina and Constantinople—, and many of the names were also unidentifiable.

As Preveza was under French occupation in the latter half of 1797, Rhigas could name contacts there without putting them in danger. A particularly significant name was that of Lavrentios Aliandros, which should rather be Algeandros, the name of a prominent local family with widespread contacts in north-western Greece. Rhigas told his interrogators, who did not believe him, that this man had sent him the texts which he combined with Khevenhüller's *Concise Theory* in his *Military Manual*: namely, the 'Democratic Catechism' and the 'imitations' of the 'Carmagnole' and 'Freut euch des Lebens'.[40] It was also to Algeandros that three boxes of revolutionary literature, which Rhigas sent in advance from Vienna to Trieste, were intended to be forwarded.[41] He was intending himself to proceed to Preveza from Trieste, and thence to the Peloponnese, in order to launch his revolution.[42]

This would have been a logical proceeding. At Preveza he would have been sure of immunity from the Turks, and perhaps also of positive help from the French. The Peloponnese, too, was a natural area to try to liberate first, as it proved to be in the revolution of 1821. But the weakness of the plan was that Rhigas seems to have had few contacts and little ready support in the Peloponnese. His close associates all came from families in the northern provinces or the islands. The letters supplied to him by the merchants in Vienna were addressed to Epiros, Thessaly and Macedonia; the letter of encouragement from Bucharest referred to friends in Thessaly, Epiros and (rather surprisingly) Athens.[43] None mentioned the Peloponnese. It has been said by a historian of the Mani that 'the Maniates were awaiting Rhigas',[44] but there is no positive evidence that Petrobey Mavromichalis had ever heard of him.

Another uncertainty concerns the klephtic leaders in all parts of Greece. Again it seems probable that his contacts were limited to the northern provinces. Names have been mentioned in Thessaly, his own homeland, such as Nikitaras and Vlachavas; to them may be added his own relative on Mount Olympus, Spiro Ziras.[45] It is probable that through Algeandros he could have made contact with the *armatoloi* of Parga, Souli, Tzoumerka and Agrapha. Two Albanian chiefs, Moukhoudar Potsa and Agou Moukhourdari, have also been named.[46] But further south all is uncertain.

In Rhigas's 'second *Thourios*' or Patriotic Hymn, he names many klephtic leaders, including some of the most famous: Botzaris and Karaiskakis in Roumeli; Kolokotronis and Zakharias in the Peloponnese.[47] But he would surely not have named in popular verses, which were intended to be on everyone's lips, men with whom he was in clandestine relations. In reality, the only slight link seems to be that Zakharias adopted a flag very similar to the one prescribed by Rhigas in the Appendix to his 'Constitution'.[48]

One other Peloponnesian was named by Rhigas: a certain religious called Cyril of Patras.[49] The phrase 'of Patras' does not imply that he lived there, only that it was his birth-place. It is therefore not impossible that this Cyril was identical with another monk born at Patras, Cyril Lavriotis, who settled at Bucharest and became, after Rhigas's death, one of his bitterest critics.[50] Rhigas did not, on the other hand, ever mention by name Dionysios Romas, a prominent figure in the Peloponnese who was alleged to be a member of his *hetairia*.[51] Nor did he name any Peloponnesian merchants. The natural inference is that he had few contacts there in comparison with the northern provinces.

Where Rhigas had contacts in mainland Greece, he seems to have felt no anxiety about recording their names. There is no evidence that they suffered any consequences, because evidently the Austrian authorities did not pass on to the Turks any names except of those whom they arrested. At Ioannina, for example, Rhigas named four men, all described as merchants.[52] He did not mention more significant figures, with whom his contacts were probable but not proven, such as Athanasios Psalidas, who was headmaster of the principal school in Ioannina; or Dr Kyritzis, who had studied medicine under the philhellene Dr J. P. Frank at Vienna, and was said by Perrhaivos to be a member of the *hetairia*. Both Psalidas and Kyritzis had some influence with Ali Pasha, the all-powerful tyrant of north-western Greece at Ioannina.[53] But Rhigas never mentioned any contact with him, if indeed he had any.

The attitude of Ali Pasha to Rhigas's movement was certainly ambiguous. Perrhaivos regarded him as a potential ally, as did the following generation of Greeks in 1821. According to Perrhaivos, quoting Psalidas, Ali Pasha later claimed to have tried to save Rhigas at the eleventh hour; but if the story is true, which is unlikely, the attempt was unsuccessful. Although Ali was also a rebel against the Sultan, he was equally a scourge of the Greeks in Albania and Epiros. Like most of the non-Turkish *pashas* in the Ottoman Empire, he had a shrewd eye for his own interest and no loyalty to anyone else. The same was true of the beys of the Levant, to whom Rhigas appealed in his *Thourios*: none of them had any inclination to rise in his support.

The one possible supporter was Pasvanoglou, whom Perrhaivos regarded as virtually a member of the *hetairia*. His name was even included in the *Thourios*, though not without a note of complaint at his inactivity. There is an informative but cryptic passage in Perrhaivos's biography of Rhigas which implies a close connection with Pasvanoglou in 1797:

> . . . if we all had his patriotic poems, that is to say the composition which he prepared and gave to Pasvanoglou, together with the written drafts by which he justified his rebellion, and also the three important documents to the great Napoleon and other correspondence with various official persons, then indeed readers would get a much clearer understanding of the magnanimity and the superior qualities of that great man.[54]

What exactly did Perrhaivos mean by the 'composition' which Rhigas gave to Pasvanoglou? Strictly construed, the word refers back to the poems, but more than that must be meant. The Greek word, which is the source of the English 'organism', can also mean a 'setting in order' or a 'system of laws'. The reference is therefore probably to the *New Political Order*. There is no evidence that Pasvanoglou ever received it. But he did rebel once more against the Sultan in December 1797, and Perrhaivos seems to have believed that he did so, remembering his past obligations, in support of Rhigas, if not in concert with him.

Modern historians doubt that Pasvanoglou would have been such a loyal ally. It is possible that the two men might have given each other mutual support if Rhigas had succeeded in launching his rebellion, but this would have been by accident rather than design. As things turned out, Pasvanoglou was at first very successful, overrunning the greater part of Bulgaria, Bosnia and Serbia, and causing alarm to the Austrians as well as the Turks. But in 1798 he was crushed by a powerful Turkish force, to which Ali Pasha contributed levies of his own. Ali would have had no hesitation in helping to crush Rhigas also, if it had been necessary. Each of the pashas was interested only in pursuing his own advantage. They would have exploited a Greek rising if it looked likely to succeed, but they would hardly have seen their pashalics as provinces of Rhigas's *New Political Order.*

In other parts of the Ottoman Empire, hardly more than a handful of Rhigas's adherents can be named. Boldness was easier for the Greeks of the northern mainland than it was for those living in or near the centres of administration and of Turkish military power, such as Constantinople, Smyrna or Belgrade. The oppressiveness of Ottoman power varied unpredictably in different places and at different times. It is remarkable, however, that apart from those arrested with Rhigas by the Austrians and handed over to the Turks as Ottoman subjects, the only Greeks whose lives he put at risk seem to have been, if the story is true, his own relatives still living in Thessaly.[55]

Presumably the reason why none of the Greeks resident in the major cities of the Ottoman Empire were compromised is that his associates were necessarily very cautious. Even so, there were a few bold spirits willing to support him. Almost all those associated with him were merchants, whose business included the distribution of books and other publications. Thus they might be drawn into patriotic activities unconsciously, and even without arousing suspicion. At Constantinople, for example, a friend of

George Poulios called Alexander Vasileiou was commissioned to forward to him issues of the French periodical *La décade philosophique, littéraire et politique.*[56] He did not know who sent them from Paris, and presumably attached little significance to them. The Austrian authorities regarded this activity with suspicion, but there is no evidence that the Turks did so. Rhigas himself named only two merchants with whom he was in touch at Constantinople, though there must have been many more. One of the two he named, Vasileios Oikonomos, was a relative and partner of Dimitrios Oikonomos, his betrayer at Trieste.[57] Other business colleagues at Constantinople included Mizanis, who had been present when Rhigas recited the *Thourios* for the first time at Vienna in September 1796. To him, or another partner, Argentis sent a copy of the *New Political Order.*[58]

At Smyrna, Argentis had another branch of his business, to which he sent much propaganda on Rhigas's behalf for circulation in Anatolia: twelve boxes containing 600 copies of the *Map of Hellas*, 50 copies each of two volumes of *Anacharsis*, and one copy of the *New Political Order.*[59] These highly compromising consignments might have been expected to convict the recipients of conscious participation in the supposed *hetairia*, but in fact there were no reprisals at all.

At Belgrade, on the other hand, there was virtually no trace of suspicious activity, whether by Greeks or Serbs. Rumour had it that Methodios, the Bishop of Belgrade, had been a member of Rhigas's *hetairia*, but that he betrayed it out of cowardice.[60] With no supporting evidence, the story can only be dismissed as a myth. It might have been believed among the Serbs of Methodios's diocese, since relations between Greeks and Serbs were often acrimonious, as is evident from the files of the *Ephimeris* at Vienna. The Serbs resented having Greek bishops imposed on them by the Orthodox Patriarchate. Only one of Rhigas's known adherents, Philip Petrovits, was of Serbian (as well as Greek) descent.

The range of the supposed conspiracy was therefore fairly limited, unless there were secret depths which have never been revealed. The authorities at Vienna were nevertheless convinced that there were ramifications of it far outside the Balkan area. They noted with concern that some of Rhigas's associates had connections with Europe. Constantine Doukas had spent time in Paris, London and Amsterdam.[61] Ioannis Mavroyenis travelled to Brussels and Paris on business. Two native-born Austrians, Kaspar Peters and Dr Frank, were in the secrets of the group. Petrovits sent a copy of the *Thourios*, translated into Serbo-Croat, to a friend or relative of the same name as himself at Leipzig; and both were ready to go to Greece and fight.[62] Anti-Ottoman pamphlets in Greek, probably printed at Leipzig, were circulating in the Danubian principalities and Bosnia.[63] The Austrians convinced themselves that they were facing an international conspiracy, animated by the French.[64]

The activities which they were actually able to ascribe to Rhigas's associates varied in seriousness. Some had merely attended parties at which his songs were sung, while he played the flute and danced round the table. Some had helped him with his publications, of which the *Anacharsis* seemed to interest the Austrians particularly. Some had read or heard excerpts from his revolutionary pamphlets. A few had declared their determination to fight in Greece. Others had expressed hostility to the monarchical system in general, including by implication the Austrian Empire itself. All were guilty of having failed to denounce the supposed conspiracy.[65] Most of Rhigas's colleagues, once they were arrested, naturally sought to diminish their complicity under interrogation. Argentis even denied any intimacy with Rhigas at first.[66] Karatzas claimed that although he had received a copy of the *New Political Order*, he was shocked by its contents and had no interest in the liberation of Greece.[67] Panayotis Emmanuel said that although he would have gone to Greece after liberation, he would not have taken part in a revolutionary war. He had spoken favourably of the French Constitution simply because it reminded him of Solon's.[68] Nikolidis similarly claimed that he only approved the French Constitution because it resembled 'the ancient constitution of Greece', but he did not approve Rhigas's *New Political Order*.[69] In most cases there was no evidence to refute these statements, but the interrogators did not believe them. Masoutis and Amoiros were more successful in exculpating themselves by turning informer.[70]

Several of Rhigas's friends could claim that their links with him were purely literary and educational. The Austrian view of these claims was arbitrary. The poet George Sakellarios, who had translated the first three volumes of *Anacharsis*, was left unmolested. Nikolidis, who was engaged on volume VII, along with other literary works relating to Greece, was arrested. George Poulios, who published the first three volumes, was also arrested, although he argued that he could not be expected to read everything he published.[71] His real crime was to have printed the *New Political Order*, but he had been told by Rhigas that it was merely a commentary on the *Map of Hellas*, so that he saw no reason to submit it to the censorship.

Others had a better case for arguing that their links with Rhigas were more cultural than revolutionary. Koronios, who was the translator of 'The First Sailor' in Rhigas's *Moral Tripod*, said that his advice to Rhigas had been to enlighten the Greeks through good books, showing 'how the Greeks were once, and how they are today, until the time should come when some neighbouring power would take pity on them and liberate them'.[72] Ioannis Emmanuel, who wrote a text-book on mathematics and gave a copy to Rhigas, similarly advised him to publish classical texts rather than revolutionary propaganda.[73] But the line between promoting emancipation and provoking revolution was no thicker than a hair, and the Austrian authorities were neither inclined nor competent to draw fine distinctions.

Two of Rhigas's associates illustrate the problem very clearly: George Poulios's brother Publius, and Dr Polyzos (also called Polyzois or Polyzoidis).[74] They were closely linked, and it was no mere coincidence that both arrived in Yassy during 1797, Poulios in April and Polyzos in July. Publius Poulios was carrying publications from the Baumeister Press for distribution, and acquiring French publications to carry back. But he was also accompanied by a group of Polish refugees, whom Rathkeal was hoping to induce the Ottoman authorities to deport back to Austria as deserters. Polyzos's intellectual interests, apart from teaching medicine and physics, were in translating excerpts from Kant and studying the French Revolution. Rathkeal also suspected him of being involved in the provision of forged Turkish passports, presumably to Greeks.[75] But it was impossible for the Austrians to lay hands on either man, since they were outside Austrian jurisdiction.

Although Rhigas shared the sympathies of all these men, to what extent he inspired them can only be a matter of conjecture. But the evidence suggests that if there was a *hetairia* such as Perrhaivos claimed, then it was very loosely organised. Modern Greek historians disagree on the subject. One wrote that Rhigas's aim was simply to 'prepare enthusiastic apostles of revolution through his books and his patriotic songs', and that he had not the organising ability to weld them into a conspiracy.[76] Another, who was himself a Marxist, disputed this interpretation and accepted Perrhaivos's picture of a conspiratorial society.[77] This was certainly also the belief of the Austrian authorities. They regarded the existence of a secret *Gesellschaft* or *hetairia* as proved by the documents which fell into their hands; and they were convinced that the French were behind it.[78]

The evidence was only sufficient to prove that Rhigas's target was the Ottoman Empire, but the Austrians saw reasons for taking the matter seriously themselves. Their relations with the Turks were for the time being friendly. They were looking for certain favours from the Porte: for example, the extradition of Polish deserters, and the grant of navigation rights off the Barbary coast. A weightier reason was fear of the contagion of rebellion. The French revolutionaries were on their own borders and in occupation of large parts of their territory in northern Europe. With French encouragement, it was thought that a successful uprising in the Ottoman Empire might easily spread to their own. They expressly recalled the abortive rebellion of Martinovicz in 1795.[79]

These reactions were certainly exaggerated. In the minds of the Greeks there was an enthusiasm for revolution but little centralised planning. Rhigas alone had a clear idea of his intention. Others knew about it in general terms, but most regarded it as a fantastic dream. In the words of his devoted young friend Petrovits: 'We want to make it possible to carry out a plan, but how?'[80] Like all the rest, he did not believe that success was possible without foreign support. Even Rhigas accepted that in his heart of hearts; but unlike most of his associates, he was prepared to make the attempt, if necessary, alone.

Was there then a *hetairia* such as Perrhaivos declared? The simplest answer is that there was not, in the sense of an organised conspiracy. Rhigas had a wide range of correspondence arising from his commercial and educational activities. As he moved from place to place, and his acquaintances did likewise, a sympathy of outlook developed between them in an unplanned and almost insensible progression. They constituted rather a fraternity than a conspiracy. Nicholas Ypsilantis spoke of a *confrérie*; and Perrhaivos also spoke in other contexts of a 'brotherhood' or 'society of brothers', recalling the traditional practice of *adelphopoiia* for mutual support and protection.[81]

These relationships spread both by personal contact and by correspondence. Rhigas had commercial colleagues and fellow intellectuals in all the major centres of the Ottoman Empire. Both he and his friends in Austria and the Danubian principalities were in correspondence with mainland Greece: with Macedonia through Torountzias, Theocharis, Doukas, Sakellarios, the Emmanuel brothers and the Poulios brothers, all of whom had family connections there; with Epiros similarly through Polyzos, Nikolidis and Algeandros; with Thessaly through Perrhaivos, Masoutis and the friends of Rhigas's childhood; with Chios through Koronios and Argentis.

There was a great deal of such correspondence, though practically none of it survives. It is easy to imagine a transition from matters of commercial or cultural business to revolutionary themes. The only letter from which an extract survives in the Austrian archives was the one from Bucharest, which tells Rhigas that 'it is no longer time for books', but he must set out for Greece to start the revolution.[82] But although the letter spoke of the Greeks 'roaring like lions', it is difficult to name more than a handful who are known by name to have been awaiting him.

The *hetairia* or *Gesellschaft* imagined by Perrhaivos and the Austrians seems, then, to have consisted of little more than a number of concentric circles, of which Rhigas was the centre. Certainly it cannot have consisted entirely and exclusively of the fifteen men arrested with him. There was a wider circle probably running at least into three figures, but tenuously connected. There was a narrower circle which could probably be counted on the fingers of one hand: perhaps only Perrhaivos, Argentis, Petrovits and Koronios can be counted as belonging to it. But Rhigas was alone in the full grasp of his mission.

[1] Kambouroglou, 101–3; Perrhaivos (1836), 19.

[2] Perrhaivos (1860), 21 and *passim*; *idem* (1836), 16, 19.

[3] Lambros (1905), 646–7.

[4] Amantos (1930), 28, 158; Legrand, 72, 100.

[5] Perrhaivos (1860), 21.

[6] *Ibid.*, 38.

[7] *Ibid.*, 26.

[8] *Ibid.*, 22 fn.

[9] *Ibid.*, 31.

[10] Amantos (1930), 154–7.

[11] Interrogation reports in Legrand, 58–111.

[12] Variously spelt in the Vienna archives: Legrand, 14–15; Amantos (1930), 28–31.

[13] Interrogation reports in Amantos (1930), 156–69.

[14] Identified with Tykas in the Vienna archives: Legrand, 2–3. See p. 99 below.

[15] Perrhaivos (1860), 24–7.

[16] Amantos (1930), 148–9.

[17] *Ibid.*, 144–7.

[18] Legrand, 74–5.

[19] I*bid.*, 96–7.

[20] *Ibid.*, 78–9.

[21] *Ibid.*, 96–7.

[22] Legrand, 44–5; 48–9.

[23] Vranousis (1953), 55.

[24] Legrand, 82–3.

[25] *Ibid.*, 46–7.

[26] *Ibid.*, 96–9.

[27] Kordatos (1974), 83–4.

[28] Amantos (1948), 396–7.

[29] Perrhaivos (1860), 24.

[30] Mikhalopoulos, 95, quoting Chiotis (1857), 12.

[31] Legrand, 76–7.

[32] Amantos (1930), 8–9; 12–13.

[33] Legrand, 108-11; 78–9; 88–9.

[34] Amantos (1930), 166–7; Legrand, 74–5; 102–5.

[35] Legrand 102–3.

[36] *Ibid.*, 46–7; 52–5; 56–7.

[37] *Ibid.*, 42–5.

[38] *Ibid.*, 72–5.

[39] *Ibid.*, 72–3.

[40] *Ibid.*, 66–7.

[41] *Ibid.*, 74–5.

[42] Amantos (1930), 6–7.

[43] Perrhaivos (1860), 22 fn.; Legrand, 72–3.

[44] Alexandrakis (1902), 46.

[45] Hertzberg, III. 289; and see pp. 6-7 above.

[46] MEE, s.v. Rhigas.

[47] Text in Papageorgiou, 41-8; Vranousis (1953), 394–7.

[48] Botzaris, 114.

[49] Legrand, 72–3.

[50] Camariano-Cioran (1974), 411–13; Amantos (1932), 54.

[51] Mikhalopoulos, 95.

[52] Legrand, 72–3.

[53] Perrhaivos (1860), 37–8.

[54] *Ibid.*, 39–40.

[55] See p. 9 above.

[56] Amantos (1930), 144–5.

[57] Legrand, 72–5.

[58] *Ibid.*, 78–9.

[59] *Ibid.*, 74–5; Amantos (1930), 88–9.

[60] Petrakakos, I. 106, citing *Neue Berlinische Monatsschrift*, May 1803.

[61] Legrand, 2–3, and n. 2 (identifying Doukas and Tykas).

[62] Amantos (1930), 15–7.

[63] Legrand, 54–7.

[64] *Ibid.*, 46-7

[65] Amantos (1930), 170–3.

[66] *Ibid.*, 16-17.

[67] Legrand, 106–7.

[68] *Ibid.*, 90–1.

[69] *Ibid.*, 84–5.

[70] *Ibid.*, 16–19; 106–9.

[71] Amantos (1930), 162–5.

[72] Legrand, 98–9.

[73] *Ibid.*, 94–5.

[74] Laios (1958), 211, 17; Hurmuzaki, XIX. 1, 814–16, 821.

[75] Legrand, 509.

[76] Amantos (1930), xiii.

[77] Kordatos (1974), 67–72.

[78] Amantos (1930), 158–9.

[79] *Ibid.*, 102–3.

[80] *Ibid.*, 126–7.

[81] Kambouroglou, 101; Lambros (1905), 647.

[82] Legrand, 72–3.

VII

VAIN HOPES IN FRANCE

RHIGAS'S colleagues recognised him as the strategist of their enterprise, but in such a widely diffused circle he could not exercise sole control over the tactics. His *New Political Order* contained a bold description of his objective. The *Military Manual*, so far as it can be reconstructed, was presumably a contribution to tactical planning. But this was a field in which Rhigas was not at his strongest, and in which others had ideas of their own. The planning of operations was in fact haphazard. Its motive force was enthusiasm rather than cool thought. How it took shape can be judged from the diary of events in 1797, culminating in Rhigas's departure from Vienna for Trieste in December.

There were at least three concurrent plans of action with different protagonists. The first was to secure the political support of the French government. Rhigas must have known about this venture, but it is improbable that he initiated it and doubtful whether he had much confidence in it. The second plan was to secure military support from the French army under Napoleon in Italy. This was clearly Rhigas's principal hope, for he rightly judged that Napoleon was a man who would take decisions on his own without too much reference to his government. The third plan was to provoke a rising in Greece through Rhigas's presence there. The second and third plans were linked by Rhigas's hope of a meeting with Napoleon, at Venice if possible, on his way to Greece. It is unnecessary to dismiss Perrhaivos's account of this intention merely because some items in the story are fanciful.

A vague formulation of the plan to secure French help can be traced earlier than 1797. An Austrian intelligence report dated 27 November 1796 spoke of negotiations between certain Greeks and the French, both in Constantinople and Paris, on the provision of French help from the army in Italy to liberate Greece.[1] The French were known to be already in touch with dissident Italians, particularly in Venice; and the fact that many Greeks were serving in the Venetian navy was thought to be a helpful factor, securing support by sea as well as by land. In return for French help the Greeks, whoever they were, offered to cede certain islands to them and to grant them a monopoly of trade.

These negotiations were said to have broken down, however, for a number of reasons. The Greeks feared that the French would insist on establishing garrisons in Greece. The French argued that it was too soon to enter into specific commitments until they had completed the conquest of Italy. They did not dismiss the project out of hand, because at the time their relations with the Turks were unfriendly. Napoleon's own correspondence shows that he himself saw some attractions in the project.

The Austrian intelligence report names only two Greeks. One was Doukas, who is called Tykas in this context—an obviously mis-spelt name which occurs nowhere else. He is said to have taken part in the approaches to the French, and was certainly involved in Rhigas's plans a year later. The other name is given as Polyzois, who was clearly Dr Polyzos. He was a principal source of the information in the report, but he can only have been unconscious that he was being exploited. The name of Rhigas is not mentioned.

There is nothing remarkable about the absence of Rhigas's name. Different Greeks at different times often made approaches on their own initiative to different powers. A group in Vienna made such an approach to Catherine the Great of Russia in 1790, when Rhigas was at Vienna; but he was not among them. It was in the same year that he made his own approach to Chancellor von Kaunitz without consulting others. In 1796 he was again in Vienna, and had already begun to circulate his *Thourios*, but he was not yet widely recognised as a national leader. It seems likely, however, that he would have known of the approach to the French, at least soon afterwards if not at the time, for Doukas and Polyzos were among his close associates. He may even have been involved in the background.

It was when Napoleon's advance across northern Italy was resumed in the spring of 1797 that Rhigas's role began to become predominant. His *Map of Hellas* and the *Thourios* gave him a unique status, which was confirmed by his bold plan for making contact with Napoleon. The *Map* was published in sections: the first sheet in 1796, three more in early 1797 (all four were seen by J. C. Engel before he sent the first volume of his *History of Hungary* to the press, for publication in the same year), and the rest by the end of May.[2] The *Thourios* was becoming more widely known from month to month.

In March Torountzias sang the *Thourios* with friends at Semlin.[3] In May Ioannis Emmanuel set out for Siatista in Macedonia with a copy, though he lost heart on the way and showed it to nobody, but often sang it privately.[4] In June Rhigas sent a copy to Koronios at Trieste, who read it out to friends there.[5] During the same period Rhigas was holding meetings with the 'more sensible and practical members of the *hetairia*' two or three times a week, according to Perrhaivos.[6] The meetings were said to be secret, but secrecy was not the Greeks' strong point. On one occasion Doukas actually read out Rhigas's 'Proclamation' to a large audience of Greeks at a café in the 'Greek Quarter' of Vienna.[7] Several of Rhigas's associates occupied lodgings close to the police headquarters.[8] Their confidence in Rhigas was unbounded.

Rhigas's own confidence was greatly stimulated by the successes of Napoleon in Italy. In April, having crossed the Austrian frontier, Bonaparte agreed to a preliminary armistice with the Archduke Charles. This was satisfactory to the Greeks of Vienna, who hoped that French arms would now be turned against their real enemy. In May there came even better news. Napoleon forced the abdication of the last Doge of Venice, who was replaced by a democratic government which invited the French to occupy the city. Thereupon the Austrians and the French shared the spoils of the Venetian Republic. The Austrians occupied Istria and Dalmatia: the French occupied the Ionian Islands and the harbours on the Greek mainland, including Parga and Preveza. On 29 June Napoleon's commander on Corfu, General Gentili, issued a historic proclamation which stirred deep emotions in the Greeks.

The proclamation was printed in French, Italian and Greek in parallel columns. It was headed 'Liberty, Humanity, Equality'—a curious deviation from the standard slogan of the Revolution. The full text read:

The French have brought liberty to Venice: the Venetians, regenerated, come in partnership with the French to restore liberty to Corfu: descendants of the first people who brought lustre to themselves by republican institutions, return to the virtues of your ancestors, restore to the name of Greece its first glory by recovering your vigour of the past.

Liberty modified by law, equality of common rights for all, respect for property, tolerance for all religions; these are the duties to which we come to recall you.

The rights in which France, the liberator of Italy, will be able to preserve you, in the name of General Bonaparte and by the will of the French Republic, the natural ally of free peoples, I assure you of great and official benefits.[9]

The spirit of the proclamation is generally attributed to the philhellene poet, A. V. Arnault, who accompanied Gentili, but he cannot be held responsible for the clumsy syntax and inaccurate spelling. There are also minor differences between the French and Greek texts. In Greek, the 'republican institutions' become 'political legislation'; and the words 'great and official' qualifying the final noun are found only in the Greek text, not in the French. But the general intention is clear. In their enthusiasm, the Greeks assumed that the proclamation was addressed to their compatriots everywhere, not merely (as was in fact the case) to the people of Corfu.

A copy of the proclamation was sent to Rhigas and Argentis from Trieste by Koronios, through Argentis's clerk Masoutis.[10] Masoutis did not immediately show it to either of them, because he was sick and absent from Vienna; but on 15 July he confirmed to Koronios that he had shown it to many Greeks. In any case Rhigas and Argentis knew of the substance of the proclamation independently. Like all Greeks, they probably read more into its text than the rhetorical phraseology would in fact justify. In the month of July there was consequently a flurry of activity, in which Rhigas was not the only actor.

While Rhigas planned to make direct contact with Napoleon, others of his group planned approaches to the French government in Paris, by two different routes. Petrovits, also a clerk to Argentis, decided on his own initiative to write a letter to the Abbé Sieyès, whom he imagined to be both sympathetic and influential. Ioannis Mavroyenis, the relative of the late Hospodar of Vallachia, planned a business journey to Paris, where he was thought to have influence in quarters which were never identified. None of these plans, unfortunately, had any fruitful consequences.

Petrovits drafted his letter to Sieyès on 17 July.[11] He wrote it in German and had a French translation made by the Austrian philhellene, Kaspar Peters. He explained touchingly in the text that it was the sole effort of an 18-year-old youth: 'I name myself so that the responsibility may be mine alone'.[12] The letter was sent on a circuitous course: first, to a friendly Austrian merchant at Basle called Elias Stinger or Steiger (whose first name suggests that he may have been half-Greek); through him to the Marquis François Barthélemy, a diplomatist, politician and nephew of the author of *Anacharsis*, who was then a member of the Directory; and through him to Sieyès in Paris.[13] Neither Sieyès nor Barthélemy, however, could have exercised much influence. Sieyès had declined to join the Directory in 1795, and Barthélemy was expelled from it by the *coup d'état* of September 1797 (Fructidor).

The German draft, but not the French translation, survives in the Austrian archives. In it Petrovits praises the military and cultural glory of France, and appeals for help of an unspecified kind. 'We are weak and oppressed', he writes; and they have no Generals such as Bonaparte and his colleagues. He leaves it to Sieyès to decide what is to be done, and asks for a reply through Barthélemy. No reply was received from Sieyès or Barthélemy, although the Austrian intermediary at Basle acknowledged receipt in a letter which Petrovits destroyed, on the advice of his fellow-clerk, Amoiros.[14]

In August Petrovits tried again. His second letter, which also survives only in the German version, appeals again for unspecified French help.[15] He hints that the alternative of Russian help, would only lead to a fresh tyranny. But without foreign help the Greeks cannot fight alone, having no weapons, gun-powder, artillery; no Generals like Hoche or Bonaparte; no officers or gunners. He argues that with French support,

> in a few days we can provoke a great uprising; then we shall capture two or three towns with a few soldiers, and when this happens all Greece will seize the sword of vengeance to overthrow the tyrant.[16]

Since the tyrants of Greece, he continues, fled even from the fire of the Germans (Austrians), 'what will you say if they hear the French artillery?' He supplies his own answer: 'With one word, our tyrants will tremble before our shadows and flee.'

But having drafted his second letter, Petrovits feared betrayal.[17] He had no translation made, and never despatched the letter, which survives only in the Austrian archives. The approach to Sieyès was never renewed. It was abandoned in favour of a more direct approach to Paris by Mavroyenis, who was about to set out in September for northern Europe on business.[18] He obtained a passport to Frankfurt in order to visit the Trade Fair. This was evidently a genuine purpose, and Argentis gave him a letter of introduction to a German merchant there. But Mavroyenis told Argentis from the first that his real destination was Paris, where he intended to contact 'men of the Directory'.[19]

Rhigas presumably knew, through Argentis, of the initiatives of both Petrovits and Mavroyenis, though he did not necessarily have confidence in either of them. Petrovits was loyal, but youthful and immature; Mavroyenis was doubtfully even loyal, as his later conduct proved. He did in fact go to Frankfurt and then to Brussels; from there he wrote to Argentis on 8 November that he was about to go to Paris;[20] and by the end of December the Austrian authorities knew that he was in Paris, planning to seek French help for the liberation of Greece.[21] His proposal was, apparently, that the French should send a force from Marseille to the eastern Mediterranean, but there is no indication to whom he put the plan.[22] The Austrians made arrangements to intercept his correspondence, and when Argentis was arrested in December they acquired the text of Mavroyenis's letter to him of 8 November. This letter clearly implied a secret mission, which enabled Count von Pergen in later years to convict Mavroyenis of lying when he denied any complicity in Rhigas's plans.[23]

Like Petrovits's correspondence, Mavroyenis's journey was entirely abortive. Rhigas would not have been surprised, because he was convinced that the key to success lay in Italy with Napoleon. Much legend surrounds his own attempts to make contact there. Perrhaivos spoke of three messages in writing which he sent to Napoleon.[24] Rhigas himself spoke of a letter which he sent in July, through Koronios at Trieste, to the French

Consul there, Captain Brechet, seeking the help of 'the General commanding in Italy'.[25] Koronios was reluctant to deliver it, but he kept it in his possession. Brechet heard early in 1798 that Rhigas, when he was arrested, had been carrying letters to himself and Napoleon, which the Austrian police had confiscated. The Austrians denied that any such letters had been in Rhigas's hands.[26] No doubt this was true, but they did not mention the earlier letter to Brechet, which Koronios had witheld and which was now in their possession. Perrhaivos was convinced, however, that communication had been established between Rhigas and Napoleon.

Some sources alleged that the two men actually met, but the chronology of their movements makes this impossible.[27] Perrhaivos gave no support to this story; he had a romantic version of his own. He writes that Rhigas sent to Napoleon a tobacco-box made from the wood of a laurel growing on the banks of the River Peneios, near the ruins of Tempe in his own native Thessaly. Napoleon was pleased with the gift, and sent a friendly reply. Rhigas then communicated all his plans to Napoleon (presumably in the documents which Perrhaivos mentioned), and Napoleon promised his support for the Greeks. When Napoleon occupied Venice, he remembered his promise and invited Rhigas to meet him there.[28] If true, this may have accelerated Rhigas's plans; but certainly no such meeting took place.

It is true that Napoleon did briefly consider a campaign in Greece. He wrote to the Directory on 26 May that it would be essential to retain permanent possession of Corfu: and on 16 August that Corfu, Zakynthos and Cephallonia were more important than the whole of Italy.[29] Between those dates he had received a flattering letter from Ali Pasha, promising his special friendship, and he had sent a party of officers to Ioannina, where they were warmly received.[30] He also had a visit from the son of Petro Mavromikhalis, Bey of the Mani, carrying a letter from his father which offered harbourage for French ships and general assistance.[31] From Gentili he heard in August that the Greeks of the Peloponnese were expecting an imminent invasion of the French.[32] He told the Directory that his contacts with the mainland led him to think that 'Greece might perhaps be reborn from its ashes'.[33]

French agents were active on the mainland at the time. Stamaty, now a French citizen, was sent by Talleyrand, the Foreign Minister, to open a 'revolutionary office' at Ancona, in order to establish communication with the Greeks and Albanians.[34] An agent in Vallachia reported in 1793 that all the merchants from Ioannina and Albania in the principality were *'sans-culottes'*.[35] They had translated the Rights of Man and knew it by heart; they were demanding revolutionary songs in order to translate them into Greek. It is tempting to suppose that these may have been contacts of Rhigas.

But neither Napoleon nor the Directory had yet made a decision. There was always a certain rhetorical ambiguity in Napoleon's language about Greece, which was echoed in Gentili's proclamation from Corfu. Arnault, who visited the mainland from Corfu, brought back in September a discouraging account of the Greeks, philhellene though he was. With the exception of the Mani, he found them degenerate and mercenary. They were 'thieves, treacherous and inhospitable, regarding every stranger only as an enemy or a prey'. Oddly enough, only the Turks looked forward to the arrival of the French: 'Liberty has no disciples except among the tyrant race'.[36]

Before receiving Arnault's report, Napoleon had commissioned another reconnaissance in the Peloponnese by Dimo and Nicolo Stephanopoli, an uncle and nephew of Greek descent, born in Corsica.[37] Dimo was a distinguished but elderly botanist, who was planning to revisit Greece in any case. Napoleon, whom he met at Milan on 30 July 1797, decided to make use of his services. As the Stephanopoli family originated from the Mani, the main object of their mission was to be the delivery of a letter to Petrobey Mavromikhalis in reply to his letter to Napoleon.[38]

Napoleon instructed them to meet Gentili in Corfu, to visit Albania and the Mani, and to report back on the results.[39] He expected them to accompany Arnault, but the latter had already left Corfu when they arrived there on 10 August. So the two Stephanopoli proceeded alone, leaving two other nephews of Dimo at Corfu. On their way to the Mani they called at Cephallonia, Zakynthos and Cythera, but apparently did not visit Albania. They landed in the Mani at Potamos, where they were met by the son of Petrobey, who was at first critical of the French; but later they were warmly received by Petrobey himself, to whom they delivered Napoleon's letter. Although carefully non-committal about Petrobey's proposal of co-operation, the letter expressed a hope for 'une bonne harmonie entre deux nations également amies de la liberté'.[40] Like Arnault, the Stephanopoli formed a favourable opinion of the Maniates, whose military exercises they witnessed. They also attended a council held by the Bey with representatives from further north: one each from Livadia (who was an Athenian), Macedonia, Crete and Albania.[41] The Bey discouraged them from trying to visit other parts of Greece, though they did land in Arcadia on their return journey. Presumably some account of their visit must have reached Rhigas, by way of the Ionian Islands.

They returned full of enthusiasm to report to Napoleon. They believed that if he himself landed in Corfu with 6,000 men, the Greeks would rise in response.[42] They suggested that his mere presence in Greece would 'extend the bounds of Greco-French liberty to the Bosporus and Thrace, to the Black Sea itself'. They hinted to the Greeks that Napoleon would come and plant a tree of freedom at Constantinople.[43] Unfortunately, however, when they arrived back at Milan, where they had parted from Napoleon, he was no longer there. Like Rhigas himself, the Stefanopoli had failed to grasp the intricacies of revolutionary politics, and in particular the tension between Napoleon and the Directory.

On 4 September 1797 the *coup d'état* of Fructidor took place in Paris, with Napoleon's connivance. He was already the predominant power in France, even from a distance. The Directory of 1795, which was relatively moderate, was overthrown and replaced by a new Directory with a Jacobin bias; it emasculated the Legislature and destroyed the last hope of a monarchist restoration. The new Directory sent instructions to Napoleon for a peace treaty which would have excluded Austria from Venice, but Napoleon simply ignored them. On 18 October, without authority from Paris, he signed the Treaty of Campo Formio, by which Austria acquired sovereignty over Venice and recognised French sovereignty in the Ionian Islands.

Thus far there was little to displease the Greeks at Vienna, though they had been hoping that he would enter the capital himself. A more disappointing consequence was that, with the

Austro-French war over, Napoleon left Italy to take up a new command for the invasion of England. He went first to Rastadt, on the Rhine, to complete the peace negotiations with the rest of the first anti-French coalition, and from there to Paris on 1 December. It did not take him long to decide, however, that the invasion of England was impracticable.

Napoleon did not immediately wipe out the Greeks from his mind's eye. One of the last orders he issued from his headquarters at Milan, on 10 November, was to Gentili to arrange for geographical and topographical studies 'from Albania to the Morea'.[44] Gentili was to study 'the situation, population and customs', and 'all the intrigues which divide these people'. He was to be particularly solicitous to the people living around Preveza, and others on the mainland opposite the French-occupied islands. All of these instructions, which would have delighted Rhigas, implied that a French campaign in Greece was still a possibility.

But French strategy, to which Napoleon contributed his own powerful advice, took another course. Once the invasion of England was abandoned, the decision was taken to cut off the British from India by seizing first Malta and then Egypt. The seizure of Malta had been recommended by Napoleon himself as early as May 1797, when he wrote to the old Directory that the island 'is of major interest to us'.[45] It was left to the new Directory to agree with him in September.

The work of the Stephanopoli was therefore in vain. They hurried north from Milan in order to report in person to Napoleon. On the way, they learned that he had left Rastadt for Paris.[46] It was therefore in December 1797 (though their *Voyage en Grèce* gives few dates) that they arrived in the capital. Dimo had some difficulty in securing an interview with the great man, but when he did so he reported that Napoleon wept to see him again. He presented his report both orally and in writing, both in Italian and in French. It covered, first, Albania, Roumeli and the Morea (Peloponnese) in general, as well as the Mani in particular; and secondly, the Ottoman Empire in general.[47] It was meticulous and full of interesting observations, but it is doubtful whether Napoleon paid much attention to it. Arnault's more pessimistic report had probably impressed him more.

In 1816, on St Helena, Napoleon lamented that he had missed

the opportunity of liberating Greece. His sentiments at that date so exactly matched the aspirations of Rhigas twenty years earlier that they still deserve to be reproduced. In conversation with his *fidus Achates*, the Comte de Las Cases, he said:

'Greece awaits a liberator! For him it would be a superb crown of glory! His name will be inscribed for ever with those of Homer, Plato and Epaminondas! I was perhaps no great distance from it! When I arrived on the shores of the Adriatic in my Italian campaign, I wrote to the Directory that I had before my eyes the Kingdom of Alexander! Later, I formed links with Ali Pasha; and when we had seized Corfu, we should have found munitions and equipment for an army of forty to fifty thousand men. I had had maps made of Macedonia, Serbia and Albania. Greece, or at least the Peloponnese, ought to fall to whichever European power holds Egypt. It should have been ours. And then, to the north, an independent Kingdom of Constantinople and its provinces would serve as a barrier to the power of Russia, just as it was alleged to do towards France by creating the Kingdom of Belgium.'[48]

Rhigas would have welcomed every word of this. He would have found Napoleon, if they had ever met, a man after his own heart.

But in reality, Napoleon's notion of liberating Greece would have been very different from that of Rhigas or the Stephanopoli, or even that of Mavromikhalis or Ali Pasha. As things turned out, the Ottoman Empire was saved from the depredations of Napoleon by his own change of course. In the eastern Mediterranean, the Ottoman Empire was saved again in 1798–99 by the victories of Nelson in Aboukir bay and of Sidney Smith at Acre. But when those battles were fought, Rhigas was already dead.

o   o   o

[1] Legrand, 2–7.
[2] Engel, I. 473–4.
[3] Legrand, 102–3.
[4] *Ibid.*, 92–3.
[5] *Ibid.*, 60–1.

[6] Perrhaivos (1860), 31; Vranousis (1953), 62.
[7] Amantos (1930), 168–9.
[8] Enepekidis (1955/b), 9–10.
[9] Petrakakos, I. 114–15.

[10] Legrand, 98–9.
[11] *Ibid.*, 124–9.
[12] *Ibid.*, 128–9.
[13] *Ibid.*, 108–9; Amantos (1930), 158–9.
[14] Legrand, 108–9.
[15] Amantos (1930), 136–7.
[16] *Ibid.*, 138–9.
[17] *Ibid.*, 158–9.
[18] *Ibid.*, 28–31.
[19] Legrand, 78–81;
Enepekidis (1955/b), 52–3.
[20] Amantos (1930), 30–1; 158–9; Legrand, 80–1; text in Enepekidis (1955/b), 40–3.
[21] Amantos (1930), 36–7.
[22] *Ibid.*, 84–5.
[23] Enepekidis (1955/b), 38 ff.
[24] Perrhaivos (1860), 39–40.
[25] Legrand, 64–5.
[26] Amantos (1930), 122–5.
[27] Mikhalopoulos, 50; Ubicini, IX (1881), 20.
[28] Perrhaivos (1860), 20–2.
[29] Bonaparte, V. 287; VI. 77.
[30] *Ibid.*, V. 350–1.
[31] *Ibid.*, VI. 75.
[32] *Ibid.*, V. 537.
[33] *Ibid.*, VI. 72.
[34] Mikhalopoulos, 93.
[35] Hurmuzaki, Sup. I, 2, 94.
[36] Bonaparte, VI. 154.
[37] Stephanopoli, I. 1–3.
[38] *Ibid.*, I. xiiij; 188.
[39] *Ibid.*, I. 75–6.
[40] *Ibid.*, I. 188.
[41] *Ibid.*, II. 71–3.
[42] *Ibid.*, II. 72.
[43] *Ibid.*, II. 84.
[44] Bonaparte, VI. 307–8.
[45] *Ibid.*, V. 45.
[46] Stephanopoli, II. 155.
[47] *Ibid.*, II. 146 ff.
[48] Las Cazes, I. 438–9.

VIII

THE GREEKS ALONE

No successor in command of the Army of Italy could be expected to show the same independence and imagination as Napoleon. Consequently, when he left Italy in the middle of November 1797, the Greeks were alone. A less heroic revolutionary than Rhigas might well have abandoned the enterprise. He could be forgiven for trying to convince his interrogators that he had done so. He told them that since Koronios had failed to deliver his letter for Napoleon to Brechet, and since he learned that the French were in friendly negotiation with the Turks, he had 'entirely abandoned his thoughts of revolution'.[1] But in fact this was not true.

He was already too deeply committed. His *New Political Order* was printed not later than 20 November, according to one of Poulios's printers; possibly even earlier, since Torountzias admitted that he received a copy from Rhigas in October.[2] About the same time, he received the letter from his friends at Bucharest telling him that the Greeks of the mainland were 'roaring like lions', and demanding to know the hour of his departure.[3] He evidently knew that Napoleon was no longer accessible. He told his friends that he now intended to go from Trieste to the Peloponnese (not to Venice), and to stir up the Mani; then to proceed north to Epiros and link the Maniates with the Souliotes; then to move into Macedonia, Albania and the rest of mainland Greece; and finally to introduce a French-style Constitution. He expected to achieve all this because the Greeks were well armed and supplied with food, and money was available from the wealthy monasteries.[4] There was no longer any talk of help from abroad.

On 1 December Rhigas received a passport for Trieste. He left Vienna on or about the 14th, having sent part of his baggage in advance and arranged for a second consignment to follow. The Austrian archives contain detailed inventories of both consignments, which clearly suggest the purpose of his journey.[5] It can be assumed that a third consignment would have followed later, because the *Military Manual*, unlike the *New Political Order*, was not yet printed.[6] Only Perrhaivos accompanied Rhigas; the rest had only supporting roles, or even none at all.

George Poulios, Argentis and Petrovits were all concerned in the despatch of the first consignment to Trieste, which was addressed to Niotis and accompanied by a letter to Koronios. The consignment was made up of four boxes: three labelled with Niotis's initials (A.N. 1, A.N. 2, A.N. 3), and one unlabelled. Their contents were meticulously recorded by the Austrian police: 144 copies of *Anacharsis* (presumably only volume IV, the latest to be published); 2,785 copies of the *New Political Order* (called, as usual, the *Proclamation*) in 109 bundles; 16 copies of the *Map of Hellas* (presumably each comprising all twelve sheets); 10 copies of the Greek New Testament; and 49 packets of pins.[7] Perhaps the one surprise in the list, apart from the pins, is the New Testament; but it was consistent with Rhigas's claim to be embarked on an Orthodox crusade.

The baggage which followed (and arrived after Rhigas's arrest) produced a more miscellaneous inventory. It consisted of two boxes labelled with the initials, G.C. 1 and G.C. 2—the Latinised form, presumably, of George Kalaphatis. The first box contained nothing more than 119 copies of *Anacharsis* and four copies of Metastasio's *Olympia* in translation (meaning presumably *The Moral Tripod*, in which the *Olympia* was the first item).[8] So far, Rhigas's baggage consisted entirely of propaganda material, obviously intended for distribution in Greece; but in the eyes of authority, the propaganda was assumed to be seditious.

The last box (G.C. 2) contained Rhigas's worldly goods, in addition to more propaganda material.[9] The inventory includes 204 maps in black and white (*scure*, in Italian): 76 coloured maps of Vallachia, Moldavia, the Archipelago, and 'Romedia' (presumably Roumeli, or mainland Greece); and 77 lithographs of Alexander the Great. The list of maps is somewhat puzzling; but since 204 is a multiple of twelve, the first bundle presumably consisted of 17 sets of the *Map of Hellas*; and since the second bundle of 76 are said to have been printed by Franz Müller, they too were evidently Rhigas's own work.

All of these items were clearly intended for distribution in Greece. There were other individual items which were not so intended, but which would have been regarded by the Austrian authorities as propaganda, and by Rhigas as purely personal and educational. The box contained, for example, several more maps and geographical works which were single items, and not Rhigas's own productions. There was a leather-bound volume containing maps, diagrams and seals of ancient Greece related to the *Anacharsis*; a *New Geography* by the Greek monk Daniel (Philippidis); a map of France in 1791; a map of Bosnia, Serbia, etc. There was a work in German on the Augustan coinage, and another German work, published in 1796, on constitutional changes. There was a work in Greek on mathematics, published in 1797, by Rhigas's friend Ioannis Emmanuel. There was a small volume in Greek, also published in 1797, by Archbishop Evgenios. There were two other unidentified books, one Greek and one French. Lastly, there was an explanatory guide to what was described as a 'historico-chronological game', with 34 maps.

The list illustrates many of Rhigas's personal and intellectual interests: history, geography, numismatics, mathematics, languages, philosophy, politics. Philippidis, the main author of the *New Geography*, was born within a year of Rhigas, also in Thessaly, and had spent four years studying in Paris soon after the Revolution. The so-called 'Archbishop' Evgenios was Evgenios Voulgaris, a learned priest but not an Archbishop. His 'small volume' was in the form of a letter replying to the work of a younger scholar, Athanasios Psalidas of Ioannina, called *Kalokinemata* (1795), which was in turn a criticism of Voulgaris's *Logic* (1766). No doubt the Austrian police regarded the whole collection with suspicion, but all it really showed was that for Rhigas the 'time for books' was still not past.

The other contents of this box were a miscellany of personal possessions. Hardly any of them could be regarded, even by hostile investigators, as implying aggressive intentions: one pistol, one oriental knife, two other knives and one brass telescope. There were one or two items of personal vanity: two portraits of himself, one an oil painting (oddly accompanied in the inventory by four wooden frames), and the other a small pen-and-ink sketch. His personal interests were served by a blue cloth bag containing his transverse flute and two other wind instruments; also a case of pens, a bottle of ink, a wooden ink-pot holder, and a lead pencil; and also two diaries, one Greek and one German, with no indication that they contained any entries.

The remaining contents provided for his health, toilet and comfort, with a touching simplicity: a thermometer, a container of unspecified white powder, a red-leather case containing four razors, a pair of scissors, and a comb; three more razors, with wooden handles; another red-leather case containing thread and spectacles; a smaller red-leather wallet containing thread and two small keys; a receptacle for salt and some chemical substance; a pair of old shoes, a pair of saddle-bags, a Greek-type water-bottle, and a feather pillow. A few private oddments complete the inventory: a pebble, a porcelain ornament, and two strings of beads (*komboloyia*), one of dark wood and one mother-of-pearl. Such was the equipment with which Rhigas set out to launch a revolution.

These starkly plain inventories tell much about his personality. They include, naturally, substantial quantities of propaganda, but nothing more deadly than that. They also include more personal clues. He collected and preserved unconsidered trifles. He had a certain concern about his personal appearance, though little about his comfort. He loved music of a simple character, which he could play on his own favourite instruments. No doubt he hardly noticed that he had lived for a few months in the same city as Haydn and Mozart; he would have appreciated, however, the esoteric symbolism of *The Magic Flute*. His passion for geography was undiminished; it was emphasised by the most recent map of France, which included the *départements* for the first time, as laid down since the Revolution.

There was, unfortunately, one other item in his baggage about which the inventory said little. This was a wallet of green cloth containing papers. It may be that these included the names, briefly jotted down, of a number of Rhigas's correspondents, in which the police naturally took the closest interest. Alternatively, he may have carried the notes on his person. In any case, it is clear that he did not have a hardened conspirator's sense of security. He had presumably not stated his exact intentions to his correspondents in writing. But he had talked about them to several of his close associates in Vienna, though not always in identical terms. Perrhaivos, for example, the only one who accompanied him when he set out from Vienna, seems to have thought that he still intended to go to Venice, hoping to meet Napoleon.[10] Others assumed that his immediate destination was Preveza, and thence to the Peloponnese.

It goes without saying that Perrhaivos was mistaken, since Venice was already under Austrian control. Preveza, however, was still in French hands; but it is impossible to guess what support Rhigas would have found there, because he had in fact already been betrayed before he and Perrhaivos set out. The circumstances are not in doubt, though the exact dates can only be conjectured.

The one certain date is that Rhigas was arrested in Trieste during the night of 19/20 December. The Governor of Trieste, Baron Brigido, reported his arrest to Count von Pergen on the 20th;[11] and Perrhaivos records that it took place during the night of their arrival.[12] Brigido reported the event post-haste, as he said, lest news of the arrest might reach the Greeks in Vienna first, and enable them to take precautions.[13]

Working back from the certainty that Rhigas and Perrhaivos arrived on the 19th, it can reasonably be estimated that they left Vienna about the 14th. Perrhaivos wrote in his *War Memoirs* that the consignment of boxes was despatched ten days before their departure: presumably about 4 December.[14] Exactly when it arrived cannot be ascertained. All that is certain is that Antonios Koronios, to whom an accompanying letter was addressed, was absent from Trieste on business in Istria. His partner, Dimitrios Oikonomos, therefore opened the letter, and was shocked by its contents. He sought advice from another local merchant, Plastaras, who was probably on the fringes of Rhigas's movement. Plastaras told him that he had no business to open private letters to his partner, and advised him to seal it up again and retain it until Koronios's return. But instead, Oikonomos took the packet to the Austrian authorities, who kept it and seized the accompanying boxes.[15]

A correction needs to be made to this account, which derives from Perrhaivos. Perrhaivos repeatedly calls the Governor 'Baron Petonki', and says that he was a Hungarian.[16] In fact there is no doubt that the Governor was Brigido. It is possible that 'Petonki' (a name repeated by the historian Philemon, probably following Perrhaivos) was a confused recollection of Pittoni, who was the Chief of Police (and evidently an Italian). This conjecture is corroborated by Perrhaivos's statement that 'Petonki' was present when Rhigas was arrested. The Chief of Police might well have been present, but certainly not the Governor.

Other corrections need to be made to Perrhaivos's account. He says that the original consignment was accompanied by letters to Napoleon as well as to Koronios.[17] Brigido mentioned in his report to Pergen two letters from Argentis to Koronios on Rhigas's behalf, but none to Napoleon.[18] He later denied to the French Consul, Captain Brechet, that Rhigas had been carrying any such letter to Napoleon either.[19] There is no trace in the Austrian archives of such a letter, whenever sent or by whatever means. It does not follow that Rhigas wrote no such letter or letters, only that none of them reached Napoleon and probably any that were written were destroyed to escape seizure.

Oikonomos's act of betrayal must have taken place while Rhigas and Perrhaivos were on the road from Vienna to Trieste. Perrhaivos says that it was 'a few days' before their arrival. That is likely enough, since if it were longer, Brigido would not have waited until after Rhigas's arrest to send a report to Pergen. It is not impossible that the two travellers were already under surveillance during the last part of their journey; but not when they left Vienna, for the authorities had the strange idea that Rhigas was on his way to the Aegean 'from a journey somewhere in Europe'.[20]

From the time of their arrival in Trieste on 19 December, the most authoritative source is Perrhaivos for the first few days, followed by Brigido and Pittoni. Perrhaivos's memory would hardly have failed him on the most dramatic episode of his life. On one curious point, however, his account is supplemented by George Kalaphatis, to whom Rhigas's second consignment of boxes was addressed. Rhigas and Perrhaivos took rooms at the Royal Hotel on the quayside. A neighbouring room, according to Kalaphatis, was occupied by the wealthy English traveller, 'Milord Hervey, Archbishop of Bristol' (in reality F. A. Hervey, Earl of Bristol, who had formerly held bishoprics in Ireland). Kalaphatis, who said he was present, added that the 'Milord' tried to intercede for Rhigas when he was arrested; but there is no confirmation of the story.[21]

According to Perrhaivos, Rhigas had intended to go to the French Consulate on the 20th, in order to seek French protection 'on the basis of a secret order from Napoleon'.[22] The last phrase

115

must have been a product of imagination; but Perrhaivos may have been right in adding that if Rhigas had gone straight to the Consulate on arrival, the Austrians would not have dared to touch him for fear of the French reaction. Brechet certainly seems to have been willing to give protection to Greeks with very slight French connections, as Perrhaivos learned a few days later.

For Rhigas himself, it was already too late. In the middle of the night 19/20 December, at about 1.0 a.m., an officer knocked on the door of their hotel room and demanded to know which was Rhigas. When Rhigas identified himself, the officer called in two soldiers, ordered them to let no one enter, and departed without another word. Perrhaivos was not at first detained, so Rhigas told him to destroy 'the secret documents of the *hetairia*'; but the soldiers prevented him. Using his diplomatic skill, and also the offer of money, Rhigas distracted their attention for long enough to enable Perrhaivos to throw the compromising documents, and also the 'seal of the nation', out of the window into the harbour waters. About an hour and a half after the first irruption, 'Petonki' (or presumably Pittoni) arrived with six officials.[23]

By Perrhaivos's account, the interrogation of Rhigas began at once, although the time was still hours before dawn. On this first occasion, the interrogators did not reveal that the boxes and letters sent in advance had already been seized. Questions were put to Rhigas alternately in French and German. Rhigas replied very briefly to all the questions, revealing only that he was on his way 'to his native land'. Perrhaivos was not questioned immediately, because he could speak only Greek: or so at least he pretended. In any case, Rhigas assured the interrogators that he and Perrhaivos were strangers to each other, who merely happened to be travelling together, and that Perrhaivos was on his way to Pavia to study as a medical student. Perrhaivos was then sent to a separate room in the hotel, and only Rhigas was kept under guard.

From the Austrian records, which never mention the name of Perrhaivos, it can be deduced that he was travelling under the pseudonym of Chrysaphis (or Christopher) Khatzivasilis. There are several references to him under that name, or simply as Vasilis, who is said to have been Rhigas's 'fellow-traveller'.[24] Evidently he used the pseudonym on other occasions, for in a collection of later correspondence between him and the schoolmaster

Andreas Idromenos on Corfu, Perrhaivos's personal seal was found bearing the Greek letters equivalent to Kh.R.Ph.S. at the top and Kh.V. below.[25] The Austrian police were suspicious of him, but apparently never established his true identity.

Rhigas's last words to Perrhaivos were to carry out as quickly as possible 'what I had not time to do'.[26] He meant that Perrhaivos should go at once to the French Consulate. Perrhaivos did so on the 20th, accompanied by a Greek serving in the Russian navy called Gabriel Palatinos, from Cephallonia. Palatinos's role in the affair is unexplained. Perrhaivos later described him as secretary to the Russian Admiral Ushakov, who commanded the force which captured Corfu from the French in 1799.[27] Presumably Palatinos was in a ship visiting Trieste in December 1797; but it is doubtful whether his company would have been of any use to Perrhaivos if the police had decided to arrest him, as they tried to do later.

Brechet, the French Consul, was a more formidable obstacle to the Austrians. Perrhaivos explained to him all that had happened, and asked for his protection on the fictitious ground that he had been born at Parga, which was under French occupation at that date. Brechet agreed, and authorised him to wear the tricolor cockade in order to warn off the police.[28] Some two weeks later the police received an order from Vienna to arrest Perrhaivos (no doubt still under his pseudonym, though Perrhaivos himself never mentions it in his own account). He was advised by Brechet to present himself to the police, but in the company of Brechet's aide-de-camp as a guarantee that he would be allowed to return. He was summoned for interrogation several times (either three or seven, according to his different versions), after which Brechet advised him to leave for Corfu.[29] He did so early in January 1798 (though in one account he mistakenly said it was before the end of 1797);[30] and at this point he ceases to be a first-hand witness to Rhigas's fate.

Meanwhile Rhigas was repeatedly interrogated, though not so thoroughly at Trieste as he was to be later at Vienna. During his third interrogation, on learning for the first time about the seizure of his poetic and other writings, he made an impassioned appeal to his interrogators, speaking warmly of Austrian civilisation, of the Emperor's humanity, and of Greece's contribution to Europe.

According to Perrhaivos, writing from hearsay, they were so deeply moved that they ended the interrogation for that day. He added, with his usual confusion of official personalities, that the Hungarian Governor was in tears.[31] In fact it is highly improbable that the Governor would have been present at such an interrogation; nor was he, and nor was the Chief of Police, a Hungarian.

One of Rhigas's chief anxieties was to avoid incriminating his friends in Vienna. While in custody, he wrote a letter to George Theocharis, a well-connected merchant in Vienna married to a German Catholic wife, urging him to approach Baron Gamerra and ask him to intervene with the authorities.[32] Unfortunately the letter fell into the hands of the police, and no doubt contributed to the arrest of Theocharis himself. Perrhaivos, however, was able to send a warning to Vienna by post, so that a number of Rhigas's associates escaped arrest for want of evidence against them.[33] It is remarkable that Brigido and Pittoni, his Chief of Police, failed to forestall this obvious step. Both of them gained little credit for their handling of the affair.

Brigido's report on 20 December prejudged the investigation by stating that Rhigas had been arrested with 'suspicious books aimed at preparing a revolution in the East'.[34] It seems very doubtful that Rhigas's literature could have been examined so quickly, since all the compromising works were in Greek. Presumably Brigido was relying on what he had been told about them by Oikonomos. The same probably applies to the letters from Argentis to Koronios, which accompanied the first consignment of boxes. Brigido added in his report that these had led him to write to his colleague Baron Thurn at Cattaro, requesting that Koronios should also be arrested.

Two days later Brigido sent a second report to Pergen.[35] Rhigas had denied any revolutionary intention, he said, but his papers showed his attachment to French ideas. He intended to distribute them widely, going first to French-occupied Preveza. Even if he only intended a revolution in the East, it could easily spread to the West, meaning Austria, where there was a large Greek population. Since his books, pamphlets and maps were printed at Vienna, Brigido suggested that it would be best to send him there for further investigation.

This report crossed a reply from Pergen, dated 25 December,

Portrait of Count Johann Anton von Pergen, Minister of the Interior
in Vienna, 1793–1804 (National Historical Museum, Athens).

to Brigido's first report.[36] He approved the measures taken, and
ordered that Rhigas and Koronios should be sent to Vienna as
soon as possible, because it was clear that the 'central organisation' was there. He said that he had arrested Argentis and others
(in fact, so far, Nikolidis, Petrovits, Masoutis and Panayotis
Emmanuel). He emphasised that he wanted the investigation to
be speedy, 'without interrupting trade, given that some of the

119

arrested merchants are involved in large businesses'.[37] This was the first indication that the Greek community was of economic importance to the Austrian state.

At the same time Pergen was also writing regular reports to the Emperor, who acknowledged them personally and asked to be kept informed. His first reports, on 25 and 26 December, were factual but prejudicial. He told the Emperor that evidently many Greeks at Vienna knew about Rhigas's revolutionary plans, and that the revolutionary documents had been prepared by Rhigas, printed by Poulios, and despatched by Argentis. He was pressing for speed in the interrogations in order to ensure that the suspects did not have time to concert their answers.

On the following days Pergen's reports to the Emperor touched on matters of policy. He wrote on 27 December that the Turkish Ambassador was being kept informed through the Ministry of Foreign Affairs, because some of those arrested were Ottoman subjects by birth.[38] The Emperor approved this irrevocable step which ultimately led to the execution of Rhigas and seven of his colleagues. Perrhaivos may have been right in believing that the Emperor hoped they would be spared, but that could only have been because he did not know the Turks.

The attitude of the Emperor was no doubt hardened by Pergen's report on the 28th, which stressed that although Rhigas's so-called *Proclamation* (the *New Political Order*) appeared to aim only at the liberation of Greece, it was full of republican slogans, which might provoke the Greeks in Austria. He added that the French were undoubtedly involved. He intended that Rhigas should be pressed 'to admit his possible relations with the French'.[39] On the 29th he stressed Rhigas's intention to establish a republic in parts of the Ottoman Empire. He also mentioned Mavroyenis for the first time as one of the conspirators.[40] On the 30th he reported that Mavroyenis had gone to Paris to seek French help in the liberation of Greece. Arrangements had been made accordingly to intercept his correspondence.[41]

As Pergen promised, arrests and interrogations were proceeding with all possible speed. Poulios was arrested on 26 December; Amoiros, Theocharis and Doukas on the 29th; Ioannis Emmanuel probably a few days after his brother. Dr Polyzos was under suspicion, but had disappeared.[42] (In fact, he had left for

Yassy many months earlier, as had Publius Poulios.) Argentis and Masoutis were the first to be interrogated in Vienna. The former admitted instructing Petrovits to despatch Rhigas's boxes to Trieste, but denied all knowledge of their contents.[43] Masoutis demolished this pretence, and was clearly willing to talk; so was Amoiros. Both of them accused Theocharis and Doukas of having republican sentiments.[44] Pergen instructed that Masoutis and Amoiros should still be held, but treated favourably. All this he recorded in a long memorandum, which seems not to have been sent to the Emperor.[45]

Another memorandum, dated 28 December but unsigned, shows the conspiratorial theory taking shape.[46] It argued, from the interrogations, that a group of young Greek hotheads from foreign universities, mostly medical students, had infected local Greek merchants with the idea of establishing 'a kind of society' (*Gesellschaft*, or *hetairia*), whose aim was to stir up revolution in Turkey. Much importance was attached to the *Anacharsis* as an instrument of propaganda, to show the Greeks how great their country had once been; also to Rhigas's so-called *Hymn of Liberty* (the *Thourios*), which he had sung at Argentis's house while dancing round the table; and to a letter of 8 November from Mavroyenis to Argentis, in which he hinted at his secret object in visiting Paris.[47] Mavroyenis's letter had been seized when Argentis was arrested; the other evidence seems to have come mainly from Masoutis.

In his report to the Emperor on 29 December, which was largely based on the preceding document, Pergen added that although the *Anacharsis* in French or German was not banned in Austria, the Greek version was 'clearly intended solely to stir up the spirit of freedom among the Greeks'.[48] The very word 'freedom' seems to have been anathema to the Austrian authorities. Consequently the *Anacharsis* was persistently treated as a seditious publication in Greek, and possession of it was virtually a proof of conspiracy. That this was their serious judgment was confirmed in 1799, when the families of two of Rhigas's fellow-victims (Karatzas and Torountzias) applied for recovery of their property. The request was granted, except for the *Anacharsis*, which was described as 'suspect'.[49] No less suspect was the *Moral Tripod*, which officials in Pergen's Ministry once called, by a revealing slip, the *'Political Tripod'*.[50]

By the end of December 1797, Pergen could congratulate himself that the investigation was going speedily and well. Ten suspects had been arrested, of whom eight were clearly implicated and two were prepared to give evidence freely. The latter two (Masoutis and Amoiros) were still kept in prison, but in privileged conditions. On New Year's day they tried to make amends for their disloyalty by asking for the release of Argentis, their employer, on the grounds that his business was being ruined.[51] This was a contingency which had already occurred to Pergen, but he could hardly agree since Argentis was incriminated by Masoutis's own evidence. On the following day Masoutis asked for the protection of the Austrian Consul at Smyrna for the firm of Argentis, and also for freedom of correspondence of the firm inside and outside Austria. To these requests, but not to the first, Pergen agreed.[52]

The hunt for suspects was still incomplete. It was impossible to lay hands on Mavroyenis, who was in Paris, or on Polyzos, who was at Yassy. But many essential facts had been extracted from those under arrest, probably under the threat of torture. Pergen reported to the Emperor on 2 January that Argentis had made significant admissions 'under pressure'. He knew that Rhigas was aiming to liberate the Peloponnese; that this was his motive in producing the maps and the translation of *Anacharsis*; and that he intended to seek foreign help, but if it were refused, to act alone. Argentis had himself given Rhigas 1,100 florins for his expenses. He refused to admit anything about the *New Political Order*, but Pergen added that the commission of enquiry would try to make him confess on this point too.[53]

More encouraging news for Pergen was also on its way from Trieste, in a report by Brigido on 29 December.[54] Koronios had been arrested at Cattaro, and was being sent to Trieste under guard. A copy of Rhigas's first interrogation report was enclosed (but the text is not extant in the Austrian archives). Arrangements were already being made to send Rhigas under guard to Vienna. Pergen was able to report to the Emperor on 6 January that Rhigas was *en route*; but his report was premature. He added that a copy of Rhigas's *Map of Hellas* had been found in Argentis's house; and that he had ordered the publication of Poulios's *Ephimeris* to be stopped.[55]

Brigido's despatch of 29 December, however, was closely followed by alarming news. On 31 December Count Pittoni, the Chief of Police, sent a note to Brigido stating that Rhigas had attempted suicide during the preceding night and had seriously injured himself.[56] Pittoni was clearly embarrassed. He explained that since the civil prison was fully occupied, Rhigas had been detained in his hotel room, where the furniture prevented complete surveillance. He had been searched, and chained hand and foot, but he had nevertheless been able to extract from his bedding a knife which, as he later admitted, he had concealed there earlier, probably during his first night at the hotel.

The bad news led to a spate of questions, excuses and recriminations, in which the Emperor, Pergen, Brigido and Pittoni all joined.[57] The Emperor demanded severe disciplinary measures, but it was never settled who precisely was to blame. There was anxiety approaching panic about Rhigas's chances of survival. On New Year's day Brigido wrote to Pergen that the wound was serious, 'but for the present we need not despair of his recovery'. The last words might be thought to have an ironic ring, but it is possible that Brigido had some sympathy with Rhigas and did not regard him as a criminal to be condemned to death. Later he had Rhigas questioned in hospital about his reason for attempting suicide, and learned that it was 'grief at being bound hand and foot'.[58] Perhaps Brigido had learned something about the Greeks for the first time.

On 4 January he reported to Pergen that according to the doctors Rhigas's wound was not dangerous. Before receiving this report, Pergen had told the Emperor on 7 January that Rhigas was 'mortally wounded', but he was able to pass on Brigido's more optimistic report on the following day. In the meantime he instructed Brigido to offer 'tempting inducements' to Rhigas to reveal 'what was the main impulse of his revolutionary plan, how far it had progressed, and above all what kind of support was expected in connection with it'.[59] Once he learned that the wound was not serious, he repeated his order to Brigido to despatch Rhigas, and also Koronios, to Vienna as soon as possible.

It was not until 18 January that Brigido could report the arrival of Koronios under guard from Cattaro.[60] By then Rhigas was recovering. According to Perrhaivos, the wound healed in a few days; he implied that he himself knew this before he left Trieste for Corfu on 7 January.[61] He attributed the failure of Rhigas's attempted suicide to the smallness of the knife, the fat on Rhigas's stomach, and the rapid intervention of the guards. The knife must indeed have been small to be so easily hidden, and Perrhaivos must have known it by sight. Rhigas's portraits confirm that he was probably overweight.

Once he was assured of Rhigas's recovery, Pergen sent instructions to Brigido on 20 January to make very secure arrangements for his transfer to Vienna.[62] Two days later he added instructions on the careful methods to be used in interrogating Rhigas while he was still at Trieste. He seems not to have had much confidence in Brigido, and intended that the chief responsibility should rest with the investigating commission at Vienna.[63] On 31 January he ordered the transfer of both Rhigas and Koronios to Vienna. They were to be kept separate on the journey; Rhigas was to be chained, but Koronios need not be.[64]

Brigido had in fact already despatched Rhigas on the way to Vienna, but not yet Koronios. He reported this in a note dated 5 February, before receiving Pergen's orders.[65] The reason for his haste was another lapse of security. Rhigas had succeeded in smuggling out a note to Brechet on 3 February, asking for the intervention of General Bernadotte, who had just been appointed French Ambassador to the Imperial Court. Brechet wrote to Brigido on 5 February complaining that he had not been allowed to see Rhigas, whom he described as claiming to have held the post of 'dragoman de la République'. He also understood that Rhigas was carrying letters to himself and General Bonaparte. He asked for these letters, and for civilised treatment of Rhigas until his status and his alleged crimes could be ascertained.[66]

An official reply was sent to Brechet stating that Rhigas had never claimed to be a 'dragoman de la République', nor was there any evidence that he had been; and there were no letters to Brechet or to Bonaparte among his papers.[67] (Although this was no doubt literally true, it overlooked the letters sent in advance by Argentis to Koronios, which were in fact already in Austrian hands.) In response to Brechet's request, however, Brigido undertook to forward his note to Bernadotte in Vienna. At the same time he hurriedly disposed of the problem by sending Rhigas on his way.

124

A photograph of the Police Headquarters in Vienna where Rhigas was imprisoned, from H. Oberhummer, *Die Wiener Polizei*, Vienna 1937 (archives of Dimitrios Karamberopoulos).

Rhigas was chained and carried in a closed van, by way of Adelsberg, Laibach, Graz, Mürzzuschlag, arriving in Vienna on the 14th or 15th.[68] At Adelsberg he made a last attempt to smuggle out a letter to Brechet, appealing for the intervention of General Bernadotte; but the letter was intercepted by his escort.[69] Koronios followed a day or two later. They were both kept at first in the Police Headquarters, which was not far from Rhigas's previous lodging. The building was relatively new, put up in 1783 on the site of a former Carmelite monastery. Its grim appearance is recorded in a photograph taken before it was demolished in 1885.[70] There Rhigas was held and interrogated until 27 April, 1798. Whether he was actually tortured is not known.

❂ ❂ ❂

[1] Legrand, 66–7.
[2] *Ibid.*, 102–3.
[3] *Ibid.*, 72–3.
[4] *Ibid.*, 70–1; Amantos (1930), 154–5.
[5] Amantos (1930), 144–9.
[6] *Ibid.*, 104–5.
[7] *Ibid.*, 148–9.
[8] *Ibid.*, 144–5.
[9] *Ibid.*, 144–7.
[10] Perrhaivos (1836), 17; *idem* (1860), 22.
[11] Amantos (1930), 2–3.
[12] Perrhaivos (1836), 17.
[13] Amantos (1930), 4–5.
[14] Perrhaivos (1836), 17.
[15] Perrhaivos (1860), 21–2.
[16] *Ibid.*, 21; 23; 26; followed by Philemon (1834), 93.
[17] Perrhaivos (1836), 17; *idem* (1860), 21.
[18] Amantos (1930), 2–3.
[19] *Ibid.*, 122–5.
[20] Legrand, 22–3.
[21] Theotokis, 39.
[22] Perrhaivos (1860), 22.
[23] *Ibid.*, 23–4.
[24] Legrand, 66-7; Amantos (1930), 108–9; 120–1.
[25] Lambros (1905), 646–8.
[26] Perrhaivos (1860), 24.
[27] *Ibid.*, 35–6.
[28] *Ibid.*, 25.
[29] Perrhaivos (1836), 18; *idem* (1860), 26–7.
[30] Perrhaivos (1860), 34.
[31] *Ibid.*, 25–6.
[32] Amantos (1930), 160–1.
[33] Perrhaivos (1860), 23 fn.
[34] Amantos (1930), 2–3.
[35] *Ibid.*, 4–5.
[36] *Ibid.*, 10–13.
[37] *Ibid.*, 8-11; 12–15.
[38] *Ibid.*, 24–5.
[39] *Ibid.*, 26–7.
[40] *Ibid.*, 32–3.
[41] *Ibid.*, 36–7.
[42] *Ibid.*, 18–19.
[43] *Ibid.*, 16–17.
[44] *Ibid.*, 34–5.
[45] *Ibid.*, 14–23.
[46] *Ibid.*, 28–31.
[47] Text in Enepekidis (1955/b), 40–3.
[48] Amantos (1930), 34–5.
[49] Laios (1958), 214.
[50] Legrand 10–11.
[51] Amantos (1930), 42–3.
[52] *Ibid.*, 88–91.
[53] *Ibid.*, 84–7.
[54] *Ibid.*, 36–9.
[55] *Ibid.*, 94–5.
[56] *Ibid.*, 40–3.
[57] *Ibid.*, 82–3; 90–101.
[58] *Ibid.*, 90–1.
[59] *Ibid.*, 94–7.
[60] *Ibid.*, 86–9; 106–7.
[61] Perrhaivos (1860), 27 and fn.
[62] Amantos (1930), 108–9.
[63] *Ibid.*, 110–11.
[64] *Ibid.*, 112–15.
[65] *Ibid.*, 118–19.
[66] *Ibid.*, 122–3.
[67] *Ibid.*, 124–5.
[68] Enepekidis (1965), 13.
[69] Amantos (1930), 130–1.
[70] Enepekidis (1965), 14–16.

IX

A STRUGGLE TO THE DEATH

WHILE the Austrian authorities awaited their prisoners from Trieste, they had subsidiary tasks in hand. There were administrative arrangements to be made, and continuing investigations to be conducted. Both of these tasks fell to Count von Pergen. More sensitive were the diplomatic implications of the plot that had been uncovered. These, which concerned relations with both Turkey and France, were the responsibility of the Chancellor, Baron Thugut (1739–1818), who was in charge of the Ministry of Foreign Affairs. He had succeeded as Chancellor when Kaunitz died in 1794. Unlike the coldly aristocratic Pergen, Thugut was a man of humble origin who had risen through the diplomatic service to the highest office entirely by his own abilities.

Pergen's first administrative decision was to suppress Poulios's Greek newspaper on 6 January 1798.[1] The *Ephimeris* had not been directly under Rhigas's influence, but it had recently supported French democratic ideas with increasing openness. As early as 1791 it had published the French 'Rights of Man'. Its subversive character had been the subject of correspondence between Thugut and Rathkeal since 1794.[2] In July 1797 the Austrian post-office at Constantinople refused to accept subscriptions to it, undoubtedly under the influence of Rathkeal. Criticism of its policies was supported even by Constantine Ypsilantis, the son of Alexander and once fellow-student with Rhigas, who became Dragoman of the Porte in 1796.[3] There was much relief among the authorities, and anxiety among the Greeks, when its licence was suspended. Six months later the Baumeister Press itself was closed.[4] By then Poulios, who had Austrian nationality, had been released from arrest and sent into exile, since he could not be deported to Turkey.

Administrative problems inevitably took up a disproportionate amount of Pergen's time. The future of Masoutis and Amoiros was a major one: they had given useful evidence against their colleagues, but they had themselves been deeply involved in the plot beforehand. Both of them were said, in counter-allegations by Argentis and Nikolidis, to have been aware of Rhigas's 'revolutionary plan', to have approved it, and to have been ready to contribute what they could to the liberation of Greece.[5] They had even been present on the first occasion when Rhigas sang the *Thourios*. As further evidence against Masoutis, the police held a letter from him to Koronios, dated 15 July 1797, saying that he had communicated 'the French proclamation' (presumably General Gentili's in Corfu) to many people, including the philhellene Dr Frank, who was very grateful for it.[6]

Nevertheless, the two informers were released and allowed to continue running Argentis's business. Amoiros was even allowed to leave Vienna for Leipzig, where he spent two months. But they were working under serious handicaps: no Greek would trust them, and their employer was in gaol. There was also the possibility that as they were Ottoman subjects by birth, the Turks would demand their extradition along with Rhigas himself and the other seven whose status was the same. This did not in fact happen, but Pergen ordered in April that they should be kept under surveillance in case they might try to abscond abroad.[7]

A more delicate case was that of Dimitrios Oikonomos, who had betrayed Rhigas and Koronios. He did nothing to mitigate his infamy. He called Koronios 'an insane criminal'; he asked for official favours in return for his treachery; and he requested on 10 January, through Brigido, that steps should be taken to protect his business partners in Turkey. A similar request was made by his brother to the Ottoman Ambassador in Vienna. The firm at Constantinople was called Mesinezis, Vlastos and Co.; and Mesinezis was actually a relative of Koronios. Brigido forwarded Oikonomos's request to Pergen, with a recommendation that it should be supported because of Oikonomos's 'patriotic' service in contributing to the frustration of the 'revolutionary plot'.[8]

Pergen replied on 19 January that he had passed the recommendation to the Ministry of Foreign Affairs, evidently with his support.[9] Rathkeal had already written favourably from Constantinople about the company in November 1797, before the plot had begun to be unveiled; and he now warmly backed Oikonomos's request. But paradoxically, though not undeservedly, it appears that these representations only had the effect of antagonising the Turkish authorities against Oikonomos and his partners even more.[10]

There were also various pecuniary matters for Pergen to settle. Brigido reported on 5 January that two of the doctors who treated Rhigas's wound had submitted excessive bills, while a third had put in a more modest account and the fourth none at all. Evidently Rhigas was already considered to be out of danger, but it is remarkable that no less than four doctors were needed to treat him. It confirms that, in Brigido's words, 'the state is so concerned for him'.[11] Nevertheless, public money must be properly dispensed; and he pointed out that the first two doctors were both state employees, whereas the other two were not. He therefore recommended substantial reductions in payment to the two official doctors, but increases to the other two. Pergen agreed in a note of 11 February.[12]

He was more forthcoming in authorising a substantial payment out of the funds confiscated from Rhigas to his fellow-traveller, who was known to the Austrians as Khatzivasilis but was in fact Perrhaivos. The latter claimed that Rhigas had owed him 300 florins; Pergen authorised the payment on 20 January in a note to Brigido, and noted on 6 February that the payment had been made.[13] There are several peculiarities about this transaction.

It seems curious, in the first place, that Pergen should have authorised the payment at all without detailed enquiries. This becomes all the more curious when it appears that the money was owed to Perrhaivos (or Khatzivasilis) for expenses in connection with the printing of the *Military Manual* (called the *Marshal Khevenhüller* in the Austrian records) at the Poulios press.[14] Presumably Pergen had no idea of the identity of Khatzivasilis; otherwise he would hardly have authorised such a payment at a time when all copies of the *Military Manual* had been seized at the press, and George Poulios himself was already under arrest.

There is also a conflict between the indubitable date of the payment to Perrhaivos and the date at which he himself claimed to have left Trieste. By his own account, Perrhaivos left for Corfu a week after Rhigas's attempted suicide, which had occurred during the night of 30/31 December.[15] He was therefore gone at least two weeks before Pergen authorised the payment to him, if his own account is correct. At that time, again according to Perrhaivos's own account, an order was out for his arrest.[16] Even allowing for bureaucratic confusion, this conjunction of circumstances seems inexplicable, except on the assumption that Perrhaivos's later accounts are not wholly truthful. It may be that his fault was only a lapse of memory, but it has been suspected that his conduct after Rhigas's arrest was not wholly blameless.[17]

After being so surprisingly open-handed towards Perrhaivos, Pergen was more niggardly over the relatively trivial matter of gratuities for the soldiers who guarded Rhigas in hospital and later on the road to Vienna. Although he had asked Brigido on 15 February to make a recommendation,[18] when the Governor's deputy, General von Saumil, did so on the 27th, Pergen said that it was excessive.[19] In the end he agreed to a smaller sum, but he pointed out that the two men had only been carrying out their official duty. He might have added that they had failed in the first case to prevent Rhigas smuggling out a note to the French Consul.

There was naturally an enquiry into the lapse of security which had enabled Rhigas to communicate with Brechet. At least half a dozen people had had contact with him in hospital, but the likeliest suspect was a Greek priest. Saumil had to report on 22 February, however, that nothing could be proved.[20] His embarrassment was diminished by being able to add that Brechet was no longer pressing the matter. But Brechet had not in fact entirely forgotten the subject. He had discussed it with General Bernadotte when the new Ambassador passed through Trieste on his way to Vienna, and he wrote a letter on 11 February to confirm their conversation.[21] His letter referred to Rhigas as 'Antoine Riga Villestindis of Zagora in Thessaly'. The Austrian records contain many equally bizarre versions of his name. Brechet reported (or rather, repeated) to Bernadotte that the letter smuggled out to him by Rhigas contained a claim to have been an interpreter at the French Consulate at Bucharest as well as secretary to the princes of Vallachia; it also claimed that he had been carrying letters addressed to Brechet himself and to General Bonaparte. Brechet added that Rhigas had gone to Vienna as a convenient place to print his maps, his Rights of Man, a republican Constitution for Greece, and proclamations to incite rebellion in Thessaly, Macedonia, the Morea and Negreponte

(Euboea); but he did not attribute this information to Rhigas himself.

He recalled that the Austrians had refused to let him see Rhigas, who had been transferred to Vienna after he had succeeded in smuggling his note out. Brechet had nothing to do with the affair personally, but he had felt obliged to write a letter on Rhigas's behalf (of which he enclosed a copy) because of his claim to have acted as an interpreter for the French. A number of nineteenth-century historians believed that Rhigas had actually succeeded in making contact with Bernadotte, but this is contrary to all the evidence.[22] In fact Bernadotte seems to have taken no action on the basis of Brechet's letters to Brigido and himself. He had other, more dramatic, ways of embarrassing the Austrian government during his brief tenure of the French Embassy.

The pursuit of conspirators and the interrogation of prisoners continued at Vienna during the first three months of 1798. The Emperor himself joined in the hunt. On 14 January he forwarded to Pergen a number of documents sent to him by the Archduke Palatine, his Viceroy in Hungary.[23] They had been seized from two Greeks arrested at Pest, Karatzas and Torountzias. Pergen reported to the Emperor on the 15th that one of the documents was Rhigas's *New Political Order*, printed at Vienna.[24] He regarded this as proof that the conspirators intended to stir up the Greeks not only in Turkey but also in the Austrian Empire. He reminded the Emperor of the conspiracy of Martinovicz in 1794–95, which had also been based at Pest.

At Pergen's request, the Emperor instructed the Archduke on the 16th to send Karatzas and Torountzias to Vienna, where they were delivered to the police on the 25th.[25] On 1 February the Emperor further informed Pergen that another Greek, Constantine Toullios, had also been arrested at Pest.[26] He was the son of a merchant, born at Pest, and therefore not liable to extradition as the other two were, since they had been born in Ottoman territory.

The tally of arrests was still not complete. In early February Dr Polyzos was arrested, not in Vienna but at Yassy.[27] He was therefore technically within Ottoman jurisdiction, but in fact under the authority of the Hospodar, Alexander Kallimakis, a patriotic

Greek who had contributed to the cost of producing Rhigas's map of Moldavia. Consequently Polyzos was not handed over either to the Turks or to the Austrians. Pergen asked the interrogators at Vienna on 13 February for details of the case against Polyzos, but the outcome is unknown and the matter was not pursued.[28] Rathkeal at Constantinople was convinced that information about the revolutionary movement could be extracted from Polyzos, but he was not to be satisfied.[29] Four months later Polyzos was released, partly thanks to the intervention of his cousin, Andreas Pavlos, a wealthy merchant at Yassy, and much to the indignation of Rathkeal.

One more arrest was still to come. Petrovits revealed under interrogation that his draft letter in German to the Abbé Sieyès had been translated into French by Kaspar Peters, who was accordingly arrested in Vienna on 23 February. In reporting this new development to the Emperor, Pergen commented that despite the characteristic deviousness of the Greeks, the truth about the 'revolutionary plan' would come out.[30] A new and disturbing feature of the latest arrest was that for the first time a native-born Austrian had been found to be involved.

By the end of February, then, Pergen had fourteen suspects under arrest, having freed Masoutis and Amoiros. The prisoners were divided into two groups, not by their degree of presumed guilt but simply by their nationality. Eight were Ottoman subjects by birth, and their names had been communicated to the Turkish authorities. A demand for their extradition had already been presented on 24 February through Rathkeal.[31] The other six, not being Ottoman subjects, were not liable to be extradited.

It is a noteworthy fact that none of the suspects was ever put on trial before a court of law, either before or after the demand for extradition. The interrogation reports on the two groups were compiled separately. Those of the Ottoman subjects were signed by the chief investigating Commissioner, J. B. Renner, and the secretary of the Commission, J. A. Fellner, on 3 April 1798;[32] those of the non-Ottoman subjects by State Councillor Ley on 18 April.[33] Among the latter was one Doukas, who was a Russian subject, but no question ever arose of his extradition.

While the interrogations proceeded, the level of activity during March was comparatively moderate. There were no further arrests, and no regular interchanges of reports between officials at Vienna. From Trieste there came lists of the contents of Rhigas's boxes: first the two boxes addressed to Kalaphatis, which were held by the police; and a week later the three boxes addressed to Niotis, which were held by the local censorship office.[34] The contents of the boxes were retained at Trieste, apart from a number of items (a hundred copies of the *New Political Order* and four of the *Anacharsis*, volume IV), which Brigido had forwarded to Pergen in early January.[35] On 29 March Pergen sent an order to Brigido to destroy all copies of the *New Political Order*.[36] No doubt he did the same in Vienna, for not a single copy of the printed text has ever been found. It survives only in manuscript; and of the *Military Manual* not even so much as that survives.

The general public in Vienna was still in the dark about Rhigas's plot and its consequences. Nothing had yet been published in the German press, nor in the Greek press; the *Ephimeris* never re-appeared after the first week of January 1798. Rumours naturally circulated among the Greek community, but it has been remarked that they kept a 'curious silence' about Rhigas in 1798 and subsequently.[37] Their caution was understandable. In the autumn of 1797, when it appeared that Napoleon's army might arrive any day in the Austrian capital itself, there had been a feeling of panic among the native-born population, whereas many Greeks looked forward to it with open enthusiasm. After the Treaty of Campo Formio in October, these emotions were sharply changed. The Greeks were subdued, the Austrians relieved. But although no proof of French complicity in Rhigas's activities was ever found, Austrian animosity towards the French was not extinguished.

One of the consequences of Campo Formio was the restoration of diplomatic relations between France and Austria. General Bernadotte (the future King of Sweden) arrived to take up his appointment in Vienna on 8 February. He took no interest in the affair of Rhigas; the nineteenth-century belief that contact took place between them is no longer to be taken seriously. The new Ambassador left his mark on Franco-Austrian relations in an emphatic way, but not by supporting domestic intrigues. An account of his undiplomatic behaviour is to be found in an unsigned letter from the Austrian Ministry of Foreign Affairs to Rathkeal, dated 17 April 1798.[38]

At 7.0 p.m. on 13 April, Bernadotte had raised on the balcony of his house in Vienna a tricolor flag with an inscription in German: *Freyheit und Gleichheit* ('Freedom and Equality'). An angry crowd gathered around, which the police drove away. They requested Bernadotte to take down the flag, which he refused to do. Then the crowd reassembled and stoned his windows. Finally the flag was torn down, and partially burned. Next day, Bernadotte demanded from the Ministry an assurance of public satisfaction. The Ministry refused without a preliminary investigation. Bernadotte then announced his intention to leave Vienna. On the 15th he was conducted out of the city with a military escort. Diplomatic relations were not actually severed, but Bernadotte's tenure had lasted barely ten weeks, and he was not soon replaced.

The same letter of 17 April to Rathkeal also contained a message which showed that Austria's official relations with the Turks were, for the present, as warm as they were frigid with the French. The message was that it had been decided to surrender Rhigas and his associates to the Ottoman Governor at Belgrade.[39] The number was originally given as ten, but it was later reduced to eight by eliminating Masoutis and Amoiros. The eight, all Ottoman subjects by birth, were Rhigas, Argentis, Koronios, Nikolidis, Karatzas, Torountzias, and the Emmanuel brothers.

The Austrians had both immediate reasons of expediency and basic reasons of principle for showing favour to the Turks. The immediate reasons were the prospect of obtaining freedom of navigation for ships flying the Austrian flag off the north African coast, and of recovering Polish deserters who had escaped to the Danubian principalities.[40] The basic reasons were the French threat to the eastern Mediterranean and the need to protect the monarchical system from revolutionary republicanism. The Turkish Ambassador in Vienna, Ibrahim Effendi, was therefore kept informed from the first about the arrests and interrogation. He promptly asked the Austrian government to hand over not only the incriminated Greeks but also the records of their interrogation.[41]

The Chancellor, Baron Thugut, sent a long memorandum on the subject to Rathkeal on 2 January. It began with a reference to

Pasvanoglou, who had launched a fresh rebellion of his own in December. His activity and intrigues, Thugut wrote, were beginning to become 'daily more threatening to the Porte'.[42] There were desertions by Janissaries to the rebels. French agents were encouraging restiveness in 'the Peloponnese and Greece'. Thugut did not expressly infer any connection between Pasvanoglou and Rhigas, but his report went straight on from the former to the latter.[43]

He wrote that indications of a plan for a Greek revolt were to be seen in 'a certain revolutionary proclamation in Greek', thousands of copies of which were found in the baggage of 'a certain Greek merchant called Rhigas Velestinlis', who had been arrested at Trieste. Many Greeks at Vienna were aware of 'the composition, secret printing and distribution of this extremely revolutionary document'.[44] The facts had therefore been communicated to the Turkish Ambassador, and Rathkeal was instructed to communicate them also to the Reis Effendi (Foreign Minister). He could at the same time raise the question of navigation off the Barbary coast.[45] He was advised against using the Dragoman, Constantine Ypsilantis, as a channel because his sincerity was suspect. It would be better to use his own First Secretary, von Wallenburg.[46]

Rathkeal replied on 25 January that he had arranged to see the Reis Effendi alone, and had asked him to preserve absolute silence on 'the Greek conspiracy'. The Minister had given him all the attention the subject deserved.[47] Rathkeal added that he would revert to the subject later, when the Reis Effendi had received the documents which were being sent by his Ambassador in Vienna. There was clear evidence of mutual good-will. Rathkeal pointed out to the Turkish Minister that Austrian troop movements had been undertaken to relieve the pressure of Pasvanoglou on Belgrade. The Reis Effendi assured Rathkeal that no credence was given by the Ottoman government to the rumour, which he had himself rebutted, that Pasvanoglou was supported by 500 Austrian artillerymen.[48]

There was naturally suspicion, both at Constantinople and at Vienna, that Pasvanoglou's outbreak was co-ordinated with Rhigas's plans. There is no evidence for this suspicion apart from the remarkable coincidence of timing. Pasvanoglou was a persistent rebel against the Sultan, always ready to take any opportunity that offered. But if he had been in contact with Rhigas, it seems more probable that he would have waited to see whether a Greek revolt had any chance of success before launching his own. A dual revolt would have been extremely dangerous for the Ottoman Empire. Even though Rhigas's plans were frustrated, the successes of Pasvanoglou on his own were remarkable for several months.

He overran large areas of Bulgaria, Vallachia and Serbia. He captured Giurgiu on the Danube, forty miles south of Bucharest, and threatened Ruschuk on the opposite bank of the river. He established a virtual blockade of Belgrade, cutting off its communications with Constantinople by land. An interesting consequence was that in March 1798 Rathkeal was obliged to send his diplomatic bag to Vienna by sea in a ship of the Royal Navy.[49] The Turks, however, eventually recovered control everywhere except in the vicinity of Vidin. Since the Greek rebellion had entirely failed to materialise, they were able to present a calm front to the European powers.

When Rathkeal next spoke to the Reis Effendi on 10 February, he found the Minister disinclined to take the 'Greek conspiracy' seriously.[50] On 24 February, however, Rathkeal reported that the Reis Effendi was demanding that all those under arrest who were Ottoman subjects should be extradited to Belgrade, saying that this was 'in accordance with the treaties'.[51] Although taken aback, Rathkeal received the information without comment. There was no such thing as an extradition treaty, but he did not ask what treaties the Minister meant.

A month later, when Rathkeal made his next visit, a new Reis Effendi was in office. Rathkeal reported to Thugut on 24 March that the new Minister, Attif Ahmed Effendi, was in a good mood.[52] He had expressed his gratitude to the Austrians for a number of acts of good will: in particular, for the information about the 'Greek conspiracy', for permitting the purchase of 1,000 Austrian rifles by the Hospodar of Vallachia, and for facilitating the export of grain to feed Turkish garrisons. These last two points were evidence that both Bucharest and Belgrade were suffering from Pasvanoglou's operations.

In general conversation, Attif emphasised the need for sovereigns to co-operate against 'the manoeuvres of innovators and men of evil intentions'; he specifically included the 'French Democrats'.[53] He also renewed his predecessor's request for the extradition of the Greek prisoners, apparently without distinguishing between those who were Ottoman subjects and those who were not. In his despatch to Thugut, Rathkeal cautiously advised in favour of compliance, 'if only as a matter of good will, and with whatever reservations Your Excellency's judgment deems necessary'.[54]

The repeated Turkish request for the extradition of the Greek prisoners presented the Austrian government with a dilemma. By the beginning of April the interrogations were complete in the case of the Ottoman subjects, but not yet in the case of the others. In neither case had there been any judicial process. In some cases the evidence of criminality was very slender: for example, Karatzas (who was an Ottoman subject, born in Cyprus). In other cases, individuals who were much more deeply involved with Rhigas's activities were exempt from extradition because they had Austrian nationality: for example, Petrovits and George Poulios. A further problem was that the interrogation of the latter group was not completed until two weeks later than that of the former.

Rathkeal had to play for time while the matter was decided. He had plenty to occupy him: fulminating against Polyzos at Yassy and Gaudin at Bucharest; against the supply of forged passports at Cherson and the circulation of Greek propaganda from Leipzig; and against the Tournavitis brothers, of whom Dimitrios had been executed by the Turks in February, but Michael was still active at Trieste.[55] But when he saw the new Reis Effendi again on 25 April, he was still unable to answer the question whether anything new had transpired about the Greek conspiracy.[56]

The discussion on that occasion was still confined to generalities. Rathkeal conveyed to Attif his government's congratulations on his appointment. Attif thanked him for the frankness shown already by the Austrian government about the conspiracy. They mutually deplored the disasters which democracy had brought to Italy and Germany, and threatened in Spain and the Kingdom of Naples. They agreed on the need for sincere understanding between conservative governments. The Reis Effendi added that 'now more than ever great monarchs must support each other and draw close together in order to oppose effectively this general political disorder.' Rathkeal concluded that it was the danger to the Aegean and to Greece, arising from the proximity of the French and the revolution in the Venetian (Ionian) Islands which made the Turks exceptionally co-operative.[57] There was apparently no reference to Pasvanoglou, whose rebellion was being gradually brought under control.

While the month of April passed with little change at Constantinople, it was different at Vienna. Apart from the fracas provoked by Bernadotte, the problem of the Greek conspirators came to a head. The report on the interrogation of the ten prisoners who were Ottoman subjects (including Masoutis and Amoiros) was submitted to Pergen on 3 April. He wrote a memorandum on the subject to Chancellor Thugut on the 7th.[58] The interrogations had shown, he said, that 'those arrested were aiming at the liberation of Greece from Turkish sovereignty'. What was to be done with the ten who were Ottoman subjects? (He noted that Masoutis and Amoiros had been left free to carry on Argentis's business.)

No record has been found of any discussion between the two Ministers, or of either with the Emperor. Perrhaivos recorded a widespread belief that the Emperor did not want to hand over Rhigas to the Turks, and would have been content to send him into internal exile. According to this rumour, the Emperor was forced to change his mind, partly out of fear of a war with France (which perhaps meant a fear that Rhigas would escape to France and provoke a renewal of the war), and partly because of threats of war from the Sultan if Rhigas were not surrendered. Perrhaivos rightly rejected these suppositions as ridiculous.[59]

An equally ridiculous story was in circulation that the Sultan promised the Emperor that the men handed over to him would not be executed.[60] The Austrians would not have believed such a promise even if it were offered. There is nothing but rumour to support such stories about the Emperor's attitude. It is clear in any case that the final decision could not have been taken without his authority. Thugut's despatch to Rathkeal on 17 April, confirming the intention to surrender ten Greeks to the Governor of Belgrade, undoubtedly had the approval of the Emperor.[61]

In fact the number to be surrendered was only eight, as

Thugut wrote on 22 April in reply to Pergen's memorandum of the 7th.[62] He pointed out that Masoutis and Amoiros had not been actively involved in the conspiracy (which was scarcely true), that they might be needed in their employer's commercial work, and that the Turks had not demanded their extradition. But he suggested that they should be kept under discreet surveillance until the Turkish government expressed its further views on the investigation.[63] The true reason for their exemption must have been their willingness to inform on their colleagues. There is nothing to show whether a revision of the number extradited from ten to eight was ever communicated to the Porte.

Thugut took advantage of his despatch of 17 April to make a bid for reciprocity from the Turks. He instructed Rathkeal to raise the question of freedom of navigation, and to press for a written guarantee that the Ottoman government would not give refuge to Polish deserters and dissidents. As an additional inducement, he enclosed a summary of the interrogation reports on the Greeks for Rathkeal's information and 'judicious use'.[64] If this was a copy of the summary which survives in the Austrian archives, it would have been an extremely valuable present to give to the Turks. It would have ended any uncertainty there might be about the ultimate fate of Rhigas and his companions. It would also have compromised many named Greeks at Constantinople, Smyrna, and towns in mainland Greece.

The authorities in Vienna gave no thought to the consequences for the latter category if Rathkeal showed the document to the Turks. But they could not ignore the problem of the six suspects held in Vienna who were not Ottoman subjects. Were they not just as guilty as those who were to be surrendered to the Turks? If they were not to be punished, that would be an implied admission that the eight were to be surrendered not because they were exceptionally guilty but simply because they were Ottoman subjects. Realistically, that was indeed the case, but it was not easily admitted.

The fate of the six could not yet be decided when Thugut sent his despatch of 17 April to Rathkeal, because the report on their interrogation was not signed until the following day. This report began, rather curiously, by summarising the case against Rhigas, under six heads: his *Thourios*, his *Map of Hellas*, his *Anacharsis* and *Moral Tripod* (counted as one item), his publication and distribution of the engraving of the head of Alexander the Great (together with the aforementioned items), his approach to the French Consul at Trieste to seek a military intervention, and his *Proclamation* (the *New Political Order*), of which he was carrying 2,000–3,000 copies with the object of stirring up a revolution in Greece. All of these accusations were said to be proved by the detailed record of the interrogations (in fact, the document signed on 3 April).[65]

When it came to the offences of the six, the document of 18 April was remarkably unconvincing. The only offence against Austrian law was Poulios's breach of the censorship in printing the *New Political Order* (which he said that he had never read). For the rest, Petrovits and Peters had intrigued with an unfriendly foreign power; the *New Political Order* and the *Thourios* were hostile to government in general; and all six were implicitly guilty of offences against their own state, both through their failure to denounce the plot and through the circulation of seditious literature against the monarchical system. But State Councillor Ley, who signed the report, gave his advice that the criminal law did not expressly provide for such cases. Penalties must therefore be left to 'the enlightened consideration of a higher judge'.[66] In passing on this advice to the Emperor on 27 April, with somewhat enhanced emphasis, Pergen suggested that the case should be submitted to a single higher judge; but possibly the best course might be to exile all six from Vienna rather than surrender them to the Turks.[67] It seems incomprehensible that Pergen should even have contemplated the possibility of surrendering six men who were not Ottoman subjects to the Turks, but in any case the Emperor resolved the matter without hesitation. He wrote on Pergen's submission: 'These individuals must immediately, without further formalities, be expelled from Austria in accordance with the above proposal.'[68] An order to this effect was issued on 28 April. They left Vienna on 10 May, destined for Leipzig.[69] On 20 June Poulios's press was compulsorily closed.[70] The fate of Rhigas and the other seven was also settled during the same few weeks. Their own admissions, added to the fact that their names had been given to the Turks, made this inevitable. The case against Rhigas has already been summarised. The admissions of the rest were equally fatal. Argentis admitted that he had known and approved Rhigas's revolutionary plan; he had read the *Thourios* and handled copies of the *New Political Order*.[71] Nikolidis made substantially similar admissions; so did the Emmanuel brothers.[72] Koronios admitted that he had passed to Rhigas extracts from the French Constitution and a copy of Gentili's proclamation.[73] Torountzias made admissions similar to those of Argentis.[74] All of them admitted that they had intended to go to Greece if the country were liberated. Karatzas was the least forthcoming; even the interrogator accepted that he knew nothing of the conspiracy, but disbelieved his claim that he had intended to denounce the *New Political Order* to the censorship.[75]

The decision communicated to Rathkeal in the despatch of 17 April was carried out ten days later. On 23 April the Ministry of Foreign Affairs received a formal note from the Turkish Ambassador requesting the surrender of the eight Greeks at Belgrade.[76] On the following day, the Ministry of the Interior sent an instruction to Field-Marshal von Kinsky for their despatch on the 27th.[77] There was to be an escort of 24 soldiers, two NCOs, and one officer. Precautions were to be taken to ensure that the prisoners did not commit suicide or escape. The escort was to consist of reliable men, and to exclude anyone belonging to the Orthodox faith. The soldiers were to receive double pay, and the officer an adequate supplement. Thugut also told Pergen that the Turkish Ambassador would send a trusted member of his staff with the party.[78] They duly departed on 27 April, though there are discrepancies between the dates given in the Austrian archives and in contemporary press reports. On 1 May Thugut wrote to inform Rathkeal, who had still not decided what he should do with the summary of the interrogation reports.[79]

❂   ❂   ❂

[1] Amantos (1930), 94–5.
[2] Laios (1958), 247–60.
[3] *Ibid.*, 211–12.
[4] *Ibid.*, 215.
[5] Legrand, 106–7.
[6] *Ibid.*, 108–9.
[7] Amantos (1930), 174–7.
[8] Lambros (1927), 170–3; facsimile of

Oikonomos's letter on plate VIII (a-b), in Enepekidis (1965), between pp. 96–7.
[9] Amantos (1930), 106–7.
[10] Enepekidis (1965), 47.
[11] Amantos (1930), 118–19.
[12] *Ibid.*, 128–9.
[13] *Ibid.*, 108–9; 120–1.

[14] Legrand, 66–7.
[15] Perrhaivos (1860), 27 fn.
[16] *Ibid.*, 26.
[17] Enepekidis (1965), 69.
[18] Amantos (1930), 132–3.
[19] Enepekidis (1955/a), 385–7.
[20] Amantos (1930), 130–1; 134-7; 140–3.
[21] Legrand, 168–9.
[22] MEE, s.v. Rhigas.
[23] Amantos (1930), 100–1.
[24] *Ibid.*, 102–3.
[25] *Ibid.*, 104–7; 114–17.
[26] *Ibid.*, 116–17.
[27] Laios (1958), 217.
[28] Amantos (1930), 130–1.
[29] Legrand, 52–3.
[30] Amantos (1930), 132–3.
[31] Legrand, 48–9.
[32] *Ibid.*, 58–111.
[33] Amantos (1930), 150–73.
[34] *Ibid.*, 144–9.
[35] *Ibid.*, 36–7.
[36] *Ibid.*, 160–1.
[37] Enepekidis (1965), 27–8.
[38] Legrand, 120-3; Enepekidis (1965), 59–61.
[39] Legrand, 118–19.
[40] *Ibid.*, 28-9; 118–19.
[41] *Ibid.*, 24-7; Amantos (1930), 24–5.
[42] Legrand, 20–1.
[43] *Ibid.*, 22–3.
[44] *Ibid.*, 24–5.
[45] *Ibid.*, 26–9.
[46] *Ibid.*, 32–3.
[47] *Ibid.*, 34–5.
[48] *Ibid.*, 36–7.
[49] *Ibid.*, 114–15.
[50] *Ibid.*, 38–9.
[51] *Ibid.*, 48–9.
[52] *Ibid.*, 54–7.
[53] *Ibid.*, 56–7.
[54] *Ibid.*, 58–9.
[55] *Ibid.*, 42–59.
[56] *Ibid.*, 134–5.
[57] *Ibid.*, 136–7.
[58] *Ibid.*, 112–13.
[59] Perrhaivos (1860), 59.
[60] Petrakakos, I. 107, citing *Neue Berlinische Monatsschrift,* May 1803
[61] Legrand, 118–19.
[62] *Ibid.*, 126–7.
[63] *Ibid.*, 128–9.
[64] *Ibid.*, 114–19.
[65] Amantos (1930), 154–7.
[66] *Ibid.*, 170–3.
[67] *Ibid.*, 178–89.
[68] *Ibid.*, 190–1.
[69] *Ibid.*, 192–3; Enepekidis (1955/b), 23.
[70] Laios (1958), 215.
[71] Legrand, 74–9.
[72] *Ibid.*, 80–95.
[73] *Ibid.*, 96–101.
[74] *Ibid.*, 102–5.
[75] *Ibid.*, 104–7.
[76] Enepekidis (1955/a), 388.
[77] Legrand, 132–5.
[78] *Ibid.*, 128–31.
[79] *Ibid.*, 142–3.

X

THE MARTYRS' SEED

So began the last journey of Rhigas and his seven companions. Leaving Vienna on 27 April 1798, they arrived at Semlin, on the Austro-Turkish frontier, six days later. The last, short stage began on 4 May, by boat down the Danube to Belgrade. There was no secrecy about it: reports of the spectacle appeared in the French and German press, evidently from the same correspondent. The eight men were chained in pairs, and still guarded by the full escort prescribed in Field-Marshal von Kinsky's orders.

Contemporary reports, whether official or journalistic, are not wholly reliable. War Office reports imply that the journney from Semlin to Belgrade took five days, which seems far too long.[1] Press reports state that only five of the eight were to be surrendered to the Turks, the other three being exiled for life.[2] In reality, all eight were handed over in Belgrade on 10 May, and lodged in the Nebojsa Tower, a grim fifthteenth-century building on the outskirts of the fortress, overlooking the Danube.

While the authorities in Vienna were thus giving full satisfaction to the Turks, in Constantinople Rathkeal was beginning to feel scruples when he learned what was taking place. On the day the eight men were handed over to the Turks, 10 May, Rathkeal had another official visit to make: not, this time, to the Reis Effendi, but to the Dragoman of the Porte, Constantine Ypsilantis, whom he naturally expected to find more sympathetic to the Greeks as well as more tactful. In contrast with Thugut, who considered Ypsilantis of doubtful sincerity, Rathkeal wrote of him as 'despite his faults and uneven temper, a basically honourable man imbued with sound principles; opposed, like his father, to democrats and revolutionaries; and linked by interest with the sounder part of his nation'.[3]

Putting Thugut's and Rathkeal's judgments together, it can be said that Constantine Ypsilantis was a typical Phanariote. But as a young man he had toyed with the idea of Greek liberation, as his father had also. It was even said that his father's resignation as

Hospodar of Vallachia in 1778 was prompted by the plans of Constantine and his brother Dimitrios to launch a premature revolution in the province.[4] Constantine's three sons all played active roles in the Greek revolution of 1821. Presumably Rathkeal did not know that the Dragoman had once been a fellow-student with Rhigas; if he did, he did not tell Thugut; but Constantine himself could not have forgotten it. Rathkeal took it for granted, in any case, that the Dragoman would not want to allow Greek emotions to be provoked throughout the Ottoman Empire by a barbarous treatment of the eight prisoners.

At their meeting on 10 May, Rathkeal made only an oral communication to Ypsilantis.[5] He witheld the summary of the interrogations which he had received from Vienna, because he was sure it would become public knowledge if he handed it over. Instead, he instructed his First Secretary, von Wallenburg, to prepare a résumé of the document, from which presumably the names of all the Greeks other than the eight surrendered at Belgrade were omitted. Rathkeal reported to Thugut on 25 May that this had been done, but no text survives.[6]

He still thought it inadvisable to present the complete summary of the interrogations to Ypsilantis, because the Greeks at Constantinople were already deeply upset by the news that Rhigas and his companions had been surrendered at Belgrade. They naturally feared for their own safety. One of them, for example, Adam Mizanis who was now back at Constantinople, had actually been present in Argentis's house at Vienna when Rhigas recited the *Thourios* for the first time; and this fact was recorded in the interrogation report.[7] Since there is no evidence that he or any other Greek at Constantinople was victimised, it can reasonably be assumed that Rathkeal evaded revealing any of their names to Ypsilantis. Most of them were merchants, and neither the Ambassador nor the Dragoman would have wished to upset trade between Vienna and Constantinople, which was mainly in Greek hands. By a not unsatisfactory irony, the only merchants who suffered hostile discrimination were the partners of the traitor, Dimitrios Oikonomos, no doubt because of the official intervention on their behalf which he had unwisely requested.[8]

Rathkeal also put in a word to Ypsilantis in favour of the eight who had been surrendered at Belgrade. He expressed the hope that the Governor there would be instructed not to subject them to further interrogation, but to send them to Constantinople, where they could be put under the charge of the Patriarch, Grigorios V. The Dragoman agreed to give advice on these lines.[9] If it had been accepted, Rhigas would still not have had an easy time, for the Patriarch abhorred revolutionaries and was the first to pour scorn on Rhigas after his death. But it was an unsuccessful manoeuvre, for communications by land between Constantinople and Belgrade were seriously interrupted by the activities of Pasvanoglou.

Ypsilantis's reactions satisfied Rathkeal, however, and he turned to other subjects which were of greater moment to his government. The first importance was attached to shipping, which took up more than half of Thugut's instructions in his despatch of 1 May.[10] But Rathkeal evidently regarded these questions as too complicated to raise orally. He decided to concentrate on the request for reciprocity on the part of the Turks in extraditing Poles and other dissidents, particularly deserters from the Austrian army. In a despatch to Thugut on 25 May, he reported that he had put the request to the Reis Efendi, who had received it with a somewhat vague acknowledgement. The importance of it, Rathkeal suggested, should now be stressed to the Turkish Ambassador at Vienna, with special reference to those who had joined rebels such as Pasvanoglou.[11]

By the end of May, Wallenburg had prepared his résumé of the interrogation reports on the eight Greeks, and presented it to Ottoman officials. Ypsilantis told Wallenburg on 31 May that he had himself been entrusted with the task of translating it, so that a decision on their treatment could be reached. He said that they had already arrived in Belgrade, and promised that the matter would be handled with 'the greatest delicacy and circumspection'.[12] In a further minute to Rathkeal on 5 June, Wallenburg reported that the Reis Effendi had expressed his gratitude for the Embassy's services in the affair, but at the same time he complained that revolutionary pamphlets were still being printed at Leipzig and distributed from there.[13]

Leipzig, the second city of Saxony, was the place to which the six non-Ottoman conspirators had been exiled. Rathkeal wrote to Thugut on 9 June to express his doubts whether the Court of

Dresden, the capital of Saxony, would be capable of restraining them.[14] It is hardly likely, however, that this particular group (although it included George Poulios, Rhigas's printer) had any hand in producing fresh propaganda so soon after the fright they had suffered in Vienna.

The Turks did not press their complaint. On the contrary, Rathkeal received a reassuring communication on 9 June to the effect that the Ottoman government would ensure the extradition of the 'criminals' wanted by the Austrian government.[15] A similar note had been received from the Ottoman Ambassador in Vienna on the previous day.[16] For the time being all was well in Austro-Turkish relations. The sequel lay in the hands of the Governor of Belgrade. By a fateful irony, Pasvanoglou, whom Perrhaivos, Philemon and others believed to have been trying to rescue Rhigas, had in fact cut the Governor's communications with the capital by occupying the passes approaching Belgrade.[17]

There were said to have been several attempts to save Rhigas and his companions. Constantine Ypsilantis no doubt did his best to secure a reprieve from the Sultan. His brother-in-law, Alexander Manos, was said to have approached the Turkish Minister of Justice with the offer of a bribe, but it proved impossible to raise the required sum of 50,000 francs in time.[18] It was also alleged that Ali Pasha wrote to the Governor of Belgrade asking him to send Rhigas to Ioannina, from where he would undertake to pass him on to the Sultan; but the Governor claimed to have received the letter too late.[19]

Perrhaivos wrote that he had heard this story from more than one source close to Ali Pasha, including the schoolmaster Psalidas. He also quoted various other Greeks who were said to have influenced Ali Pasha, including Dr Kyritzis, a former student under the philhellene Dr Frank at Vienna and supposedly a member of Rhigas's *hetairia*. But Perrhaivos discounted the story as improbable, pointing out how foolish it would be for any Greek to place any trust in Ali Pasha.

Perrhaivos gave more credence to the story of Pasvanoglou's attempt to intervene by force:

When he heard of the tragic events that had befallen Rhigas, and the final decision that had been taken against him, Pasvanoglou occupied all the public highways and tracks, and the Danube, with an armed force to rescue his saviour and guide from peril. Then the Pasha of Belgrade, being unable to convey the condemned men to Constantinople, received new orders to execute them at Belgrade.[20]

Other sources assumed that he received no such orders, but took the decision himself.

The story of Pasvanoglou has a romantic plausibility. At one time he certainly had held Belgrade in the grip of a virtual blockade. But by the summer of 1798 the Turks were already gaining the upper hand. At the end of June, the month in which the executions took place, the Military Governor of Semlin, Colonel Schertz, reported to Vienna that Pasvanoglou was reduced to a state of siege in Vidin, though the Turks did not dare to make a direct assault on the well-fortified town.[21] His blockade of Belgrade must therefore have been broken some time earlier; and Perrhaivos's story cannot be taken seriously.

The same report from Colonel Schertz, dated 28 June, stated that the Governor of Belgrade had received orders from Constantinople to execute his prisoners on the spot. This he was said to have done by having them strangled, in great secrecy, at night on 24 June. He then put out a rumour that they had escaped, and sent out search-parties in a pretence of pursuit. Part of the story was confirmed by a report in the *Neueste Weltkunde* on 18 July.[22] The journal's correspondent added that some people thought they had been executed, but he considered it more probable that they had in fact escaped. He was wrong; but whether Colonel Schertz was also misinformed about the order from Constantinople or the method of execution remains unknown.

There is no trustworthy, independent account of Rhigas's death. The only possible sources would necessarily be Turkish. A Turk was still living at Belgrade in 1875 who claimed to have been one of Rhigas's guards, and even to have taken part in his execution, but his claim was clearly fictitious. On the other hand, he might have drawn on the same source as Perrhaivos, since both attributed to Rhigas much the same dying words, and both agreed that they were spoken in Turkish. The old Turk's version was: 'Thus giants die. I have sowed, others come who will reap.'

Perrhaivos's version is more elaborate: 'Thus heroes die. I have sowed seed enough; the hour will come for it to sprout, and my race will gather the sweet fruit.'[23]

Nothing more in the old Turk's story is worth repeating, for it is full of nonsense and self-contradiction. Perrhaivos's account of his friend's death is the only one that can be regarded as even remotely probable, since other versions are no more than repetitions or variations of it. The Turkish Governor, according to Perrhaivos, pretended that the prisoners were to be sent to Constantinople by boat down the Danube. He ordered that they should be taken out of the prison one by one, and then drowned in the river. Rhigas was the last to be despatched. When a guard tried to seize him by force, Rhigas gave him such a violent blow that he fell to the ground 'half-dead'. The Pasha then ordered that Rhigas should be shot in prison, and thrown dead into the river so that the Greeks should never find his body and bury it. Two Turkish soldiers were sent into his cell with pistols; it was they who heard his last words before they shot him.[24]

Until Colonel Schertz's report was received, the authorities in Vienna appear still to have believed that Rhigas would be sent alive to Constantinople. Their naive trust in Turkish clemency is shown by a despatch sent from the Ministry of Foreign Affairs to Constantinople on 19 June, less than a week before Rhigas and his companions were executed in Belgrade, and far too late for any intervention.[25] The despatch was prompted by the news of Napoleon's new expedition in the Mediterranean. He had sailed from Toulon on 19 May, and occupied Malta on 10 June. The Austrians were seriously perturbed by the uncertainty of his destination.

Would he aim for Egypt? Would he occupy Crete? Was there still to be an uprising in Greece? In order to answer these questions, the Ministry's despatch instructed Rathkeal to request a fresh interrogation of Rhigas and his companions by the Turks. The theory of collusion between Napoleon and the Greeks died hard. It was rumoured that there had been a meeting between them before the Treaty of Campo Formio; it was even held, in an anonymous German publication of 1824, that Napoleon's Egyptian expedition had actually been jointly planned with Rhigas.[26] Serious scholars throughout the nineteenth century—Gervinus,

Leake, Hertzberg, Mendelssohn-Bartholdy, François Lenormant —persisted in believing that Rhigas had succeeded in making contact at least with Bernadotte, if not with Napoleon in person. But all these stories belonged to the realm of fantasy; and the last despatch from Vienna to Constantinople about Rhigas, on 19 June 1798, was merely the crowning ineptitude of a disgraceful proceeding.

So Rhigas slipped away into legend, as he had emerged from legend in his youth. It does not affect the legend whether he was strangled or shot or drowned. In any case, the bodies of himself and his companions were never found. As with other legends, the details of his legend also disappeared for many years. As recently as 1916 an eminent Greek historian had to admit that Rhigas's real name was still unknown;[27] even his date of birth was unknown until the Austrian archives became available in 1890. In the meantime serious efforts were made to discredit him and to bury his name in obloquy. These began in the very year of his death, under the influence of the Patriarch Grigorios V.

Grigorios launched a series of attacks on Rhigas, direct and indirect, in 1798. First came the *Paternal Instruction*, for which he did not acknowledge personal responsibility. It was composed, if not by himself, certainly by a writer with his authority; but it was published under the name of the Patriarch of Jerusalem, who was thought to be on his death-bed.[28] The Patriarch of Jerusalem, however, recovered and denounced the work as none of his own. As was customary at the time, it did not name Rhigas, but it attacked the 'atheistic French' and all supporters of nationalist and republican ideas. The first prominent Greek to respond was Korais in Paris, with his *Fraternal Instruction*, published anonymously in Rome. He did not name either Rhigas or the Patriarch, but his subject and his target were perfectly clear. He denounced the Austrian Emperor for 'pitilessly surrendering to the tyrant of Greece eight Greeks who were trying peacefully to enlighten their compatriots and to liberate them from the yoke of slavery'; and the unnamed author (as distinct from the innocent Patriarch of Jerusalem) he called 'an implacable enemy of the religion and the name of the Greeks'.[29]

Other obedient ecclesiastics took up the chorus. One of them, the Protopsaltis Iakovakis of Constantinople, appended some verses to the *Paternal Instruction* commending subservience to Ottoman rule. Some typical couplets read:

Let each remain in that state to which he has been called;
Let him not gainsay the kingdom to which he is subject.

From the first beginning the world was subjected
To one first Lord, and so it has ever been.

Let us submit ourselves faithfully to our sovereign,
Not acting according to foreign examples in any way.

To these lines also Korais responded with militant verses of his own.[30]

The Patriarch was not to be put to shame. Two more denunciations followed under his own name. In December 1798 he addressed an Encyclical to the Metropolitan of Smyrna, and another to the Metropolitan of Paros and Naxos, each of which had a wider circulation. Again he did not name Rhigas, but he expressly attacked the *New Political Order*, giving the pamphlet its correct title in full, and adding that it was written in 'simple Romaic'. The identification was clear, and showed that Rhigas's work had been in circulation despite the efforts to suppress it. The Patriarch ordered that all copies should be collected and sent to him at once, and no one should be allowed to read it because 'it is full of corruption through its deceitful notions, and contrary to the doctrines of our Orthodox faith'.[31]

Grigorios also sent emissaries to the Peloponnese and other parts of Greece to emphasise his message. Rhigas was named as the target for the first time in 1801, by the Metropolitan of Ioannina in a message to the people of Parga, warning them not to be misled by Perrhaivos and stating that those executed had deserved the sentence of death by which they were punished by God.[32]

Korais was for some years the only prominent writer who supported Rhigas's patriotic principles, but he did so always obliquely without naming him. He wrote a War Hymn of his own in 1799, and another poem called the 'Trumpet Call' in 1801, which was once mistakenly attributed to Rhigas. But poetry was not Korais's true medium. His most effective propaganda was through his scholarly editions of the Greek classics, which carried on Rhigas's conviction that education was the high road to freedom. He was too cautious to encourage his countrymen openly to follow Rhigas's example of armed rebellion.

Illustration by a nineteenth-century popular artist of Korais and Rhigas rescuing Greece from the ruins of her past glory (National Historical Museum, Athens).

In those years Rhigas's name was rarely mentioned among the Greeks. The first to write about him was George Zaviras, in a work called *New Greece, or Greek Theatre;* but although it was written about 1804, it was not published until 1872. The first published book to name him was the anonymous *Greek Rule of Law, or Discourse on Liberty*, which appeared about 1806. The author, who was possibly Ioannis Kolettis, a future Prime Minister, wrote as dedication: 'To the grave of the great and ever memorable Greek Rhigas, who was sacrificed for the salvation of Greece, the writer offers this small work as a gift in gratitude.'

More was probably written about Rhigas at this time in French or German than in Greek. Germans and Austrians were especially sensitive about his fate. In 1803 a short, anonymous biography appeared in the *Neue Berlinische Monatsschrift* compiled from 'the papers of a man who has lived for a long time in the Turkish Empire'.[33] It was well informed, though not without errors. In 1804, J. C. Engel published the fourth volume of his *History of Hungary* containing a reference to the tragic fate of Rhigas, whom he had known personally, and mentioning his map of Moldavia.[34] By a strange chance, in the same year, the maps of both the Danubian principalities were reprinted at the request of the Ottoman Ambassador to Vienna (who was, as so often, a Greek, Constantine Typaldos).[35]

In official circles, however, Rhigas's name was still anathema. To have been associated with him was disastrous, as Ioannis Mavroyenis found at the turn of the century. He had read in 1798 the account of Rhigas's fate in the *Neueste Weltkunde*, which linked his own name with the conspiracy. At his insistence, the journal published a denial of its own report. He then wrote to a senior official at the Imperial Court on 3 January 1799, repeating his denial of the story in circumstantial terms. He claimed that he had only known Rhigas, Argentis and Nikolidis casually in the course of the notorious law-suit against Baron Langenfeld some years earlier. He took the opportunity to request permission to return to Vienna from his exile in the Rhineland.[36]

In reporting the matter to the Emperor, Count von Pergen exposed a tissue of lies in Mavroyenis's letter, quoting from documents in the state archives. Among them was Mavroyenis's letter to Argentis on 8 November 1797, showing that he was then on his way to Paris for a clandestine purpose.[37] Pergen therefore advised that Mavroyenis should be debarred from returning to Vienna, and the Emperor agreed. The ban lasted until 1811, when by an extraordinary reversal of fortune Mavroyenis was nominated as Ottoman Ambassador to the Imperial Court, and accepted as such.[38]

Other more respectable exiles were rehabilitated with less delay. Theocharis was allowed to return to Vienna from Leipzig in 1806, and George Poulios in 1808. The surviving documents on their cases show that they had made good reputations for themselves in business abroad.[39] The others exiled in 1798 were also allowed to return.

The only associate of Rhigas who never returned to Vienna, though not officially an exile, was Perrhaivos. After his escape to Corfu at the beginning of 1798, he stayed there for some time as a teacher, with his friend Andreas Idromenos. Then he travelled restlessly across Europe—to Paris, back to Parga, to Odessa, to Moscow—until the formation of what he called the 'second *hetairia*' and the revolution of 1821 gave him a new purpose in life, which he amply fulfilled. Unfortunately in the course of his wanderings he lost all his documents, some to a British naval patrol in 1811 and some to the Turks in 1825.[40] So his published writings, in 1836 and 1860, depended entirely on his memory, which was not always accurate. But his correspondence with Idromenos survived, and provided a valuable supplement to his record.[41]

Still more valuable to posterity was his publication of two of Rhigas's most famous poems, both probably printed at Corfu in 1798 or soon after. They are to be found in two very rare booklets, one containing the *Thourios*, and the other containing the 'Hymn to Napoleon' (not by Rhigas, but perhaps by Perrhaivos himself) and the 'Patriotic Hymn' ('All the nations go to war...'), which Perrhaivos called the 'second *Thourios*'. These booklets were found among Idromenos's papers in Corfu.[42] According to Perrhaivos, the *Thourios* and the 'Patriotic Hymn' were the only poems correctly ascribed to Rhigas; and his testimony is not to be underrated.[43]

Most of Perrhaivos's contemporaries accepted not only these two but many other poems as Rhigas's work, including the so-called 'Paean' or 'Greek Marseillaise', which Byron translated as 'Sons of the Greeks, arise!' It is reported that in 1814 a collection of poems ascribed to Rhigas was published at Yassy, but no copy of it is known to survive.[44] There were also manuscript copies of his poems in circulation, and many references to their popularity as songs before and during the Revolution of 1821. The first foreign publication of the *Thourios* was in Fauriel's *Chants populaires* of 1824. Fauriel recorded that a Greek friend of his had met a boy working in a bakery about 1817, who could not read but had hidden on him a book of Rhigas's poems, which he asked every passing traveller to read out to him, while he listened with tears of emotion.[45] The book may have been a copy of the publication in 1814 at Yassy.

Thus it was Rhigas's poetry which kept his name alive. It had to compete, however, with the slanders of his critics. The bitterest of them was Michael Perdikaris, who had known him at Bucharest in their youth. About 1806 Perdikaris wrote a long satire in verse called *Demokritheraklitos* (a title taken from Voulgaris's *Logic*), which was not published until 1817.[46] In it he attacked every imaginable target, both progressive and reactionary, including Rhigas and his tutor Katartzis. He also wrote in 1811 a more personal attack on Rhigas as one of the 'pseudophilhellenes', vilifying his character and acquitting Oikonomos of blame for having denounced him, which was 'the salvation of the whole Greek race'.[47] This work was written at Vienna, where it was examined by the censorship but never published. The reason may have been either that the censor of Greek, Bartholomew Kopitar, was sympathetic towards Rhigas, or that the finance for publication was not forthcoming.[48] Still, Perdikaris was respected among contemporary intellectuals, including Rhigas's friend Sakellarios and the learned Archimandrite, Anthimos Gazis, who arrived in Vienna shortly before Rhigas's arrest, and even Ioannis Kapodistrias, who knew Perdikaris as a student in Italy.[49]

Another severe critic of Rhigas was Cyril Lavriotis, the monk from Patras who settled at Bucharest.[50] He spent many years from 1817 compiling a vast *Interpretation of the Apocalypse*, in which he denounced Rhigas as an atheist. 'Rhigas, the man of troubled spirit', he wrote, 'perished miserably, as befits a miserable man.'[51] He did not, however, like other ecclesiastics, oppose in principle a rebellion against Ottoman rule; he even believed it would succeed, but not if it depended on foreign support. He therefore also attacked the younger Alexander Ypsilantis, for relying (vainly, as it turned out) on Russian support for his foray into the Danubian principalities in 1821. In Cyril's eyes, this was a repetition of Rhigas's error in relying on the French.

But the rising of 1821 was also a repetition of other aspects of Rhigas's vision. The founders of the *Philiki Hetairia* were consciously reforming the *hetairia* which they believed that Rhigas had formed. Some of its leading figures also shared his aim of liberating not merely Greece but the whole Balkan peninsula. The three Ypsilantis brothers, grandsons of Rhigas's first patron, must have heard of his character and aspirations from their father, Constantine. Nicholas, the least-known of the three brothers, shows in his *Memoirs* that he was familiar with at least parts of the *New Political Order*. He was the most effective in organising the revolution, and he must have influenced the strategy adopted by his brothers.

The strategy might have been directly inspired by Rhigas's maps and his *Thourios*. It comprised a simultaneous pincer operation on the northern and southern extremities of the Balkans. Alexander was the leader in the north, entering the Danubian principalities from Russia with the support of Romanian nationalists. Dimitrios was to lead the southern uprising in the Peloponnese. Subsidiary outbreaks were to be stimulated in Thessaly, Macedonia, Epiros, Albania, and if possible in Bulgaria and Serbia; but the decisive action was to be in the northern and southern arms of the pincer. The leadership of the Ypsilantis brothers was expected to ensure Russian support.

But circumstances foiled the attempt. No Russian aid was forthcoming. The Romanian patriots, although they sang Rhigas's songs as they marched on Bucharest, wanted to be rid of their Phanariot Hospodars rather than of Ottoman sovereignty. The initial outbreak degenerated into a war of attrition for the liberation of Greece alone. But it was launched, unmistakably, on the basis of a strategic theory derived from Rhigas.

The revolution of 1821 naturally revived memories of Rhigas, though he still had critics as well as admirers. The first sympathetic biography by a Greek was published in French by Constantine Nikolopoulos in 1824;[52] and a poem in his honour, 'Le tombeau de Rhigas', was composed by Auguste Bonjour in 1826.[53] On the other hand, an early history of the revolution, also by a Greek writing in French, Rizos Neroulos, was severely critical. His view in 1828, before independence was assured, was that:

When one contemplates the abyss into which Rhigas was about to precipitate Greece, it is impossible not to groan and deplore not so much his project in itself as its ill-timed and ill-planned execution.[54]

At about the same date another Greek composed, again in French, a loving forgery called the *Last Farewells of Rhigas*. Although certainly not authentic, it bears the imprint of Rhigas's favourite ideas, expressed in successive admonitions to the people, the rulers, the men of learning, the merchants and seamen, the clergy, and finally the whole nation of Greeks. Characteristic phrases show that the author was familiar with Rhigas's thought. He stresses the vital role of education; he alludes to the *Anacharsis* and to the legend of Tantalus; he tells the clergy that their responsibility is not only to God but to their fatherland; and he tells the nation that 'the dawn already presages the day of your political resurrection'.[55]

The manuscript of the *Last Farewells* was found in Corfu among the papers of Ioannis Kapodistrias, who ruled Greece from 1828 until his assassination in 1831.[56] With the manuscript was found a paper containing notes on Rhigas, based on information supplied by George Kalaphatis, who had been at Trieste when Rhigas was arrested there.[57] Evidently Kapodistrias had been interested in the *Last Farewells*, and had asked for a personal brief on its hero. The writer of the brief described Rhigas as 'easily moved to enthusiasm rather than to deliberation; and one could not call this venture of his hopeful so much as desperate'.[58] He wrote in Italian, and was therefore presumably an Ionian Greek who knew Rhigas personally.

Judgments of Rhigas continued to fluctuate after Greece won her independence. In 1833 a tragedy on his fate was written by I. Zambelias. In 1834 Ioannis Philemon wrote ambiguously of him in his 'Historical Essay on the *Philiki Hetairia*':

> He was a man of great ideas and enterprise, but neither prudent nor discreet; he possessed much learning and a lively spirit, but he was a superficial judge of affairs.[59]

His reputation stood higher, in fact, as a literary pioneer than as a political figure. In 1836 the first play staged in a modern Greek theatre was the translation of Metastasio's *Olympia*, attributed to Rhigas in the programme.

A shift of opinion began with the publication of the memoirs of participants in the War of Independence, especially those of Perrhaivos in 1836 with a preface largely devoted to Rhigas. Still more impressive, ten years later, were the words of Kolokotronis in the preface to the last edition of his *Memoirs*: 'Rhigas Pheraios stood as the great benefactor of our race; the ink of his pen will be precious in the eyes of God, as the blood of the saints.'

By the middle of the century his memory was restored in many ways, especially in verse. The Italian poet Luigi Mercantini praised him as 'profeta e martire' in a poem of 1851. The Bavarian philhellene Friedrich Thiersch wrote a Greek epigram to him and his companions in three elegiac couplets.[60] Many Greek poets celebrated him: notably George Zalokostas (1805–58), Julius Typaldos (1814–83), and above all Kostis Palamas (1859–1941). But the numerous biographies added little to Perrhaivos's *Short Biography* (1860) until Legrand's discoveries in the Vienna archives.

Statues were erected to him, first outside the University of Athens (ironically, alongside the Patriarch Grigorios V, who had denounced him, but became a martyr in his turn in 1821); and others later at Velestino, Volos and Belgrade. Visual relics of him also came to light: his signature on the wall of a Viennese café;[61] and many portraits, of which the first in England was published in 1859.[62] About 1850 a French traveller saw his *Map of Hellas* on the wall of a Greek school in Turkey;[63] and towards 1900 and after, the maps of Moldavia and Vallachia and the engraving of the head of Alexander, long thought lost, were rediscovered.

A major advance in the interpretation of Rhigas's life and character was the publication in 1860 of Perrhaivos's *Short Biography*. Despite its imperfections, it provided an essential basis for future studies. Anastasios Goudas drew extensively on it for his account of Rhigas in the second volume of his *Parallel Lives* (1874), in which he significantly classified Rhigas in the company of Voulgaris, Korais and other intellectuals under the general heading of 'Education'. But two more landmarks had to be passed before Rhigas could enter the realm of documented history.

In 1881 a manuscript was found in Zakynthos containing the Greek text of the 'Proclamation', the 'Rights of Man', and the 'Constitution', which made up the *New Political Order*.[64] In the same year, Thessaly was annexed to the Kingdom of Greece as a belated consequence of the Congress of Berlin in 1878. Rhigas's homeland was thus simultaneously laid open to scholarly investiga-

Statue of Rhigas by John Kossos outside Athens University, erected
at the expense of George Averof in 1871.

tors, among whom N. G. Politis pioneered the collection of anec-
dotal data on Rhigas's childhood from local reminiscences (though
naturally no one was still living who had ever set eyes on him).

A second equally important landmark was the work of the
French historian, Émile Legrand, who gained access in 1890 to
the files on Rhigas's interrogation, and those of his companions, in
the Austrian State Archives. Here again was found, in German
translation, the greater part of the *New Political Order*, with the

Statue of Patriarch Grigorios V by George Phytalis outside Athens
University, erected at the expense of George Averof in 1872.

exception of the first 13 articles of the 'Rights of Man' and the last
ten of the 'Constitution'.[65] Legrand's pioneering work was continued in the next century by K. Amantos and P. K. Enepekidis,
among other scholars working in the Vienna archives.

The rediscovery of Rhigas has continued at intervals in the
twentieth century. In 1924 his prose translation of Metastasio's
Olympia, which had served in 1790 as the basis for a verse translation by another hand, was published for the first time.[66] It was

not until 1930 that the *Last Farewells of Rhigas* was found and published, though the editor recognised that it could not be by Rhigas's hand. Of his adaptations, it was not until 1945 that his *School of Delicate Lovers* was recognised as derived from Rétif de la Bretonne's *Les Contemporaines*;[67] and not until 1955 that Khevenhüller's *Kurzer Begriff* was identified as the source of his *Military Manual*.[68] Since it was as recently as 1962 that a new manuscript of the *New Political Order* was discovered at Bucharest, it may be surmised that other discoveries may still be possible in future.[69]

Meanwhile, it is pleasant to record an honourable act of penance in 1930, when the Mayor of Vienna officially gave Rhigas's name to a street near the place where he had lodged. It bears the inscription:

Konstantinos Rigas Pherräos
1754–1798
griechischer Freiheitsdichter

There are admittedly mistakes on the plaque: the first name is wrong, and so is the date of birth. But Rhigas would have been happy to be recognised as a 'Poet of Freedom'. Contemporary Greeks were also pleased by the Viennese Mayor's acknowledgment that the purpose of the plaque was 'to wipe out a historic act of wrongdoing', for which he blamed 'the monarchical sentiments which then prevailed'.[70]

For the Greeks, naturally, Rhigas is more than a 'poet of freedom'. He symbolises many aspects of the rebirth of their country. He is the 'proto-martyr' (a title once reserved for St Stephen). He is a liberator, even if only in the imagination. He is the national hero whose name is adopted by heroic causes. In 1877 a secret society called *Pheraios* was part of the impetus which swept the Greeks into an unofficial alliance with Russia against Turkey, leading four years later to the acquisition of Rhigas's native Thessaly.[71] In another context, the name Rhigas Pheraios was chosen by the secret society of university students which fought the military dictatorship of 1967–74. They had his statue at the entrance to the University of Athens to encourage them.

His name typifies, for liberal Greeks, the primacy of educational and cultural emancipation, as well as constitutional and

Woodcut by Vaso Katraki from *Agones tou Ellinikou Laou* [*Struggles of the Greek People*], circulated in 1943 by the Greek resistance group ELAS-EAM (archives of Dimitrios Karambelopoulos).

social reform. He represents these things for all Greeks, but also other things for others among them, For conservatives, he is the self-made businessman who was also the nationalist patriot, while for Marxists he represents the bourgeois capitalism which characterises the emergence of national consciousness from aristocratic feudalism. For them, too, he stands as the pioneer of Balkan supranationalism which is destined one day to emerge from national chauvinism,[72] a role which is symbolised by the statue put up to him at Belgrade, although he never set foot in the city except on his way to a martyr's death in June 1798.

How much of this would have astonished him? He was a man of simple self-expression, but he had strong convictions. Two of his sayings illustrate both this simplicity and the strength of these convictions: first, 'whoever reasons freely, reasons well'—words which survive in his own handwriting in the manuscript of the *Anthology of Physics*;[73] second, 'from letters is born the progress with which all free peoples shine'—his own addition to article 22 of the 'Rights of Man'.[74] The word 'free' is the link between them.

But freedom does not come about of its own accord, as his revolutionary *Thourios* proclaimed. Rhigas was a revolutionary who deplored the necessity for violent revolution, but saw no other way. His instinct told him that reason and letters alone could not bring about revolutionary change. It told him also that, even if his revolutionary action failed, as it did, the seed he sowed would yield a harvest to be reaped by others, as after many years it was.

◊ ◊ ◊

[1] Legrand, 170–3.
[2] *Neueste Weltkunde,* 3 June 1798; *Moniteur,* 10 June 1798.
[3] Legrand, 148–9.
[4] MEE, s.v. Alexander Ypsilantis.
[5] Legrand, 146–7.
[6] *Ibid.,* 150–3.
[7] *Ibid.,* 76–7.
[8] Enepekidis (1965), 47.
[9] Legrand, 152–3.
[10] *Ibid.,* 136–43.
[11] *Ibid.,* 152–7.
[12] *Ibid.,* 158–9.
[13] *Ibid.,* 158–61.
[14] *Ibid.,* 162–3.
[15] *Ibid.,* 164–5.
[16] *Ibid.,* 160–1.
[17] Perrhaivos (1836), 18; *idem* (1860), 28; Philemon (1834), 94.
[18] Neroulos (1828), 139–40.
[19] Perrhaivos (1860), 37–8.
[20] *Ibid.,* 28.
[21] Legrand, 166–7.
[22] Enepekidis (1965), 48–9.
[23] Legrand, ii–iii; Perrhaivos (1860), 28.
[24] Perrhaivos (1836), 18–19; *idem* (1860), 28.
[25] Amantos (1932), 40, citing D. Pantelić.
[26] Vranousis (1953), 89; MEE, s.v. Rhigas, citing *Anon.* (1824).
[27] Lambros (1916), 69.
[28] Makraios, in Sathas, III, 394; Clogg (1969), 87–115.
[29] Korais (1798), 18–19; 29–33; 64; Kordatos (1974), 147.
[30] Korais (1798), 37–9; Clogg (1969), 106–8.
[31] Pappadopoulos, II. 498–9; Daskalakis (1962), 12 n. 2.
[32] Kordatos (1974), 148 n. 3; Kitromilidis (1990), 38.
[33] NBM, May 1803, 381–8.
[34] Engel, IV. 69.
[35] Enepekidis (1965), 34.
[36] Enepekidis (1955/b), 20–1; 42–7.
[37] *Ibid.,* 40–3; 50–3. For quotations

from *Neueste Weltkunde*, 3 June 1798 and 18 July 1798, see *ibid.*, 48–51.

[38] *Ibid.*, 38–41; 52–7.

[39] *Ibid.*, 28–30; 60–71; 94–111.

[40] Perrhaivos (1860), preface to 1971 edition, ix–xii; *ibid.*, 18.

[41] Lambros (1905), 642–7.

[42] *Ibid.*, 648–50; Daskalakis (1937), 27–9; Vranousis (1953), 389–97.

[43] Perrhaivos (1860), 12–18.

[44] Vranousis (1948), 9–10; Kordatos (1974), 61.

[45] Fauriel, II. 18.

[46] Dimaras (1974), 174.

[47] Amantos (1948), 400.

[48] Enepekidis (1960), 4–5; 74–9.

[49] Dimaras (1974), 174; MEE, s.v. Perdikaris.

[50] Camariano-Cioran (1974), 411–13.

[51] Dimaras (1974), 169.

[52] Legrand, i, fn.

[53] Enepekidis (1955/a), 401–2.

[54] Neroulos (1828), 138.

[55] Theotokis, 1–15 (French original); 16–30 (Greek translation).

[56] *Ibid.*, v–viii.

[57] *Ibid.*, 37–9.

[58] *Ibid.*, 40.

[59] Philemon (1834), 90.

[60] Perrhaivos (1860), 41.

[61] Vranousis (1953), 399.

[62] Lambros (1905), 625–31; Xenos, I, facing p. 33.

[63] Ubicini, VIII (1881), 241.

[64] Daskalakis (1937), 34.

[65] Amantos (1930), 44–83.

[66] Daskalakis (1937), 15.

[67] Thomopoulos (1950), 1028–38.

[68] Enepekidis (1955/a), 388–96.

[69] Daskalakis (1962), 16.

[70] Petrakakos, I. 117.

[71] Dakin, 129.

[72] Kordatos (1974), 14.

[73] Vranousis (1953), 399.

[74] See p. 70 above.

BIBLIOGRAPHY

Greek, Russian and Serbo-Croat titles are transliterated into Latin script.

Section I lists Rhigas's works, in chronological order so far as this can be established, with the principal editions identified briefly in brackets.

Section II lists the principal editors and commentators, in alphabetical order, expanding the abbreviated identifications in Section I.

References in the footnotes are confined to the editors' or authors' names and dates, as identified in these and the following sections of the bibliography. The date is omitted if only one work by a particular author is listed. The abbreviation MEE stands for *Megali Elliniki Engkyklopaideia - Great Greek Encyclopaedia*.

I RHIGAS'S WORKS

Scholeion ton ntelikaton eraston (Vienna 1790); ed. Vranousis (Athens 1953), 114–98; Pistas (Athens 1971)..

Physikis apanthisma (Vienna 1790); ed. Vranousis (Athens 1953), 249–87.

Prophiteia tou makariou ieromonakhou Agathangelou (?Vienna 1791); ed. A. Politis (Athens 1969), 173–92.

Megali kharta tis Ellados (Vienna 1796–97); ed. Laios (Athens 1960); sections reproduced in Vranousis (Athens 1953), 359–68; complete set reproduced by the Cultural Institute of the Agricultural Bank of Greece, with texts in Greek and English (Athens, 1993).

Geniki kharta tis Moldavias (Vienna 1797); ed. Laios (Athens 1960).

Nea kharta tis Vlakhias (Vienna 1797); ed. Laios (Athens 1960).

Eikon tou Megalou Alexandrou (Vienna 1797); ed. Laios (Athens 1960).

O ithikos tripous (Vienna 1797); ed. Vranousis (Athens 1953), 289–328, omitting 'O protos navtis'.

To taxidion tou neou Anakharsidos, IV (Vienna 1797); ed. Vranousis (Athens 1953), chapters 35–9, with omissions.

Nea politiki dioikisis (Vienna 1797; no printed copies extant); reconstruction in Daskalakis (Paris 1937; Athens 1962); also in Vranousis (Athens 1953), 369–88, and in Papageorgiou (Athens 1971), 9–38; English translation in Clogg (London 1976), 149–63.

Engkolpion stratiotikon (Vienna 1797; no copies extant); see Daskalakis (Paris 1937), 36–7.

Dimokratiki katikhisis (Vienna 1797; no copies extant); see Daskalakis (Paris 1937), 37–8.

Thourios (ed. C. Perrhaivos, Kerkyra, ?1798); with French translation in

164

Fauriel (Paris 1824), II 20–9; ed. Daskalakis (Paris 1937), 62–71; Vranousis (Athens 1953), 389–93; Papageorgiou (Athens 1971), 5–8; incomplete English translation in Dalven (New York 1949), 65–7.

Ymnos patriotikos (ed. Chr. Perrhaivos, Kerkyra, ?1798); also in Vranousis (Athens 1953), 394–7; Papageorgiou (Athens 1971), 41–8.

Paian i ethnikos ymnos (ed. Hobhouse, London 1813), II 586–7; Iken (Grimma 1827), II 103–5; Papageorgiou (Athens 1971), 49–52.

II EDITIONS AND COMMENTARIES

A. B. Daskalakis: *Les oeuvres de Rhigas Velestinlis* (Paris 1937).

——: *To politevma tis Ellinikis Dimokratias tou Rhiga Velestinli* (Athens 1962).

P. Khiotis: 'I nea politiki dioikisis tou Rhiga', in *Parthenon*, 1871, 506–12 and 545–56.

G. Laios: 'Oi khartes tou Rhiga', in *Deltion tis istorikis kai ethnologikis etaireias tis Ellados* (new series), 14, 1960, 231–312.

G. T. Papageorgiou: *I Elliniki dimokratia* (Athens 1961).

P. S. Pistas: 'Ta tragoudia tou engkolpiou tou Rhiga', in *Ellinika*, 22.1, 1969, 183–206.

——: *Scholeion ton ntelikaton eraston* (Athens 1971).

A. Politis: 'I prosgraphomeni ston Rhiga proti ekdosi tou Agathangelou: to mono gnosto antitypo', in *Eranistis*, 7, 1969, 173–92.

A. Ubicini: 'La grande carte de la Grèce par Rhigas', in *Revue de Géographie*, 8, 1881, 241–53; *ibid.*, 9, 1881, 9–25.

T. P. Volidis: *To politevma tou Rhiga* (Athens 1929).

L. I. Vravousis: *Symvoli stin erevna yia ta tragoudia tou Rhiga kai ton mimiton tou* (Athens 1948).

——: *Rhigas – erevna, synagogi kai meleti* (Athens 1953).

——: *O 'Patriotikos ymnos' tou Rhiga kai i elliniki 'Karmaniola'* (Athens 1960).

——: *Ekdoseis kai kheirographa tou 'Scholeiou ntelikaton eraston'* (Athens 1970).

III DOCUMENTARY SOURCES

K. Amantos: 'Nea engrapha peri tou Rhiga Velestinli', in *Praktika tis Akadimias Athinon*, II, 1927, 305–312.

——: *Anekdota engrapha peri Rhiga Velestinli* (Athens 1930).

N. Bonaparte: *Correspondence inédite officielle et confidentielle: Italie* (Paris 1819).

P. K. Enepekidis: 'Ekthesis peri ton televtaion erevnon peri Rhiga Velestin-li', in *Ellinika*, supplement 9, 1955, 385–403 (cited as 'Enepekidis, 1955/a').

——: 'Symvolai eis tin istorian ton syntrophon tou Rhiga', in *Thessalika chronica*, 6, 1955, 1–124 (cited as 'Enepekidis, 1955/b').

——: 'Wiener Untersuchungsakten aus dem Jahre 1793 einer griechischen angeblichen Spionageaffaire', in *Ellinika*, 14.2, 1956, 373–417.

——: *Symvolai eis tin mystikin pnevmatikin kinisin ton Ellinon tis Vien-nis pro tis epanastaseos* (Berlin 1960).

M. I. Gedeon: *Kanonikai diataxeis* (2 vols., Constantinople 1888–89).

É. de Hurmuzaki: *Documente privitoare la Istoria Românilor,* Sup. I (3 vols., Bucharest 1885–89).

P. Iliou: *Prosthikes stin Elliniki vivliographia: ta vivliographika katalogia tou É. Legrand kai tou H. Pernot* (1515–1799), (Athens 1973).

J. Kabrda: *Quelques firmans concernant les relations franco-turques lors de l'expédition de Bonaparte en Égypte*, 1798–99 (Paris 1947).

A. Korais: *Allilographia* (6 vols., ed. C. Th. Dimaras, Athens 1964–84).

G. C. Ladas and A. D. Khatzidimos: *Elliniki vivliographia 1791–1795* (Athens 1970), and *1796–1799* (Athens 1973).

J. Lair and É Legrand: *Documents inédits sur l'histoire de la révolution française* (Paris 1872).

S. Lambros: 'Erevnai en vivliothikais kai arkheiois', in *Neos Ellinomnimon*, 21, 1927, 170–3.

É. Legrand: *Documents inédits concernant Rhigas Velestinlis et ses com-pagnons de martyre* (Paris 1892; in German, French and Italian, with a Greek translation by Sp. Lambros).

D. Pantelić: *Pogibija Riga iz Fere* (Belgrade 1931).

G. G. Pappadopoulos and G. F. Angelopoulos: *Ta kata ton aoidimon pro-tathlitin tou ierou ton Ellinon agonos Patriarkhin Konstantinopoleos Grigorion E´* (2 vols., Athens 1865–66).

Sp. Theotokis: *Oi televtaioi khairetismoi tou Rhiga* (Athens 1931).

IV BIOGRAPHICAL STUDIES

K. Amantos: *Rhigas Velestinlis: nea vivlia peri avtou* (Athens 1932).

J. C. Bolonachi: *Hommes illustres de la Grèce moderne* (Paris 1875), 1–38.

A. Dimitrakopoulos: *Prosthikai kai diorthoseis eis tin Neoellinikin Philolo-gian K. Satha* (Leipzig 1871).

I. Dragoumis: *Apo ton vion kai to ergon tou Rhiga* (Athens 1912).

B. E. Edmonds: *Rhigas Pheraios, the Protomartyr of Greek Independence* (London 1890).

P. K. Enepekidis: *Rhigas – Ypsilantis – Kapodistrias* (Athens 1965), 11–96.

A. N. Goudas: *Vioi paralliloi ton epi tis Anagenniseos tis Ellados diaprep-santon andron,* II (Athens 1874), 109–44.

G. Laios: *O Varonos Langenfelnt kai o Rhigas Velestinlis* (Athens 1955).

S. Lambros: *Apokalypseis peri tou martyriou tou Rhiga* (Athens 1892).

P. Mikhalopoulos: *Rhigas o Velestinlis, 1757–1798* (Athens 1930).

K. Nikolaidis: *Istoria tou Ellinismou* (Athens 1923), 246–52.

C. Nikolopoulos: *Notice sur la vie et les écrits de Rhigas* (Paris 1824; an extract from *Revue encyclopédique,* February 1824; also in M. Ray-baud, *Mémoires sur la Grèce,* II (Paris 1825), 488–94.

N. I. Pantazopoulos: *Rhigas Velestinlis – i politiki ideologia tou Ellinis-mou; proangelos tis epanastaseos* (Thessaloniki 1964).

Chr. Perrhaivos (1836): *Apomnimonevmata polemika* (ed. E. G. Protop-saltis, Athens 1956), preface, 16–19.

———— (1860): *Syntomos viographia tou aoidimou Rhiga Pheraiou* (ed. A. Kharisis, Athens 1971).

K. Sathas: *Neoelliniki philologia* (Athens 1869), 529–40.

G. Theophilos: *Viographia Rhiga tou Pheraiou* (Larisa 1887).

C. Valamoutopoulos: *Rhigas o Pheraios* (Athens 1891).

L. I. Vranousis: *Rhigas – erevna, synagogi kai meleti* (Athens 1953).

————: *Rigas – un patriot grec din Principate* (Bucharest 1980).

V SPECIALIST ARTICLES

K. Amantos: 'Oi Argentai tis Chiou', in *Chiaca chronica,* IV, 1919, 83–119.

————: 'Rhigas Velestinlis', in *Ellinika,* 5, 1932, 36–60.

————: 'Rhigas Pheraios', in *Nea Estia,* 43, 1948, 396–400.

Anon.: 'Über die Verschwörung einiger Griechen in Wien in Jahr 1797', in *Neue Berlinische Monatsschrift,* 9, 1803, 381–8.

G. L. Arsh: 'Rigas Velestinlis—grecheskii revolutioner-demokrat', in *Balka-nskii istoricheskii sbornik,* I, 1968, 34.

————: 'Les premiers échos de la grande Révolution Française dans les Balkans (1793–1797)', in *Report of Conference* at *Institut National des langues et civilisations orientales,* Paris, 1988, 31–48.

————: 'Velikaya Phrantsuzskaya Revoliutsiya i Balkanii', in *Novaya i Noveishaya Istoriya,* Moscow, 5, 1989, 40–54.

————: 'L'influence de la Révolution Française dans les Balkans', in *Études Balkaniques,* Sofia, 1, 1991, 34–39.

N. Camariano: 'Contributions à la bibliographie des oeuvres de Rigas Velestinlis', in *Balcania,* I, 1938, 224–7.

A. Camariano-Cioran: 'Les îles Ioniennes de 1797 à 1807 et l'essor du courant philofrançais parmi les Grecs', in *Praktika tou tritou Panioniou synedriou*, Athens, 1967, I, 83–114.

———: 'L'activité d'Émile Claude Gaudin, premier consul de France à Bucarest', in *Revue Roumaine d'Histoire*, 9.2, 1970, 251–60.

R. M. Clogg: 'A further note on the French newspapers of Istanbul during the revolutionary period', in *Belleten*, 155, 1975, 483–90.

———: 'The Dhidhaskalia Patriki (1798)', in *Middle Eastern Studies*, 5, 1969, 87–115.

N. Corteze: 'La Valachia durante il Principato di Alessandro Ypsilanti', in *L'Europa Orientale*, II.3, 1922.

A. Duţus: 'Ethics, Scherzi and Delectation', in *Balkan Studies*, 13, 1972, 265–77.

A. Elian: 'Conspiratori greci in Principate', in *Revista Istorică*, 21, 1935, 337–72.

A. Elian: 'Sur la circulation manuscrite des écrits politiques de Rhigas en Moldavie', in *Revue Roumaine d'Histoire*, I, 1962, 487–97.

N. Iorga: 'O scrisoare a lui Rigas', in *Revista Istorică*, 1.2, 1915.

———: 'Vienne comme centre des idées de l'Occident et de l'esprit révolutionnnaire', in *Revue historique du Sud-Est Européen*, I, 1924, 23–26.

D. A. Karamberopoulos: 'Iatrikes gnoseis tou Rhiga Velestinli sto ergo tou *Physikis Apanthisma*', in *Hypereia*, I, 1986, 457–99.

O. Katsiardi: 'Ellinika diavimata ston Bonaparti', in *Eranistis*, 14, 1977, 36–68.

P. M. Kitromilides: 'Politikos oumanismos kai diaphotismos: symvoli sti dierevnisi tis ideologikis leitourgias tis politikis theorias tou Montesquieu', in *Philosophia kai Politiki*, 1982, 291–304.

S. V. Kougeas: 'Ti epire mazi tou o Rhigas erkhomenos eis Ellada', in *Nea Estia*, 43, 1948, 401–2.

L. Lagarde: 'Notes sur les journeaux français de Constantinople à l'époque révolutionnaire', in *Journal Asiatique*, 236, 1948, 271–6.

G. Laios: 'Oi adelphoi Pouliou, o Georgios Theokharis, kai alloi syntrophoi tou Rhiga', in *Deltion tis istorikis kai ethnologikis etaireias* (new series), 12, 1957, 202–70.

S. Lambros: 'Simeiomata peri Rhiga kai Perrhaivou', in *Miktai Selides* (Athens 1905), 623–53.

———: 'O Rhigas kai i elliniki paroikia tis Viennis', in *Logoi kai anamniseis ek tou vorra* (Athens 1909), 55.

———: 'Rhigas, Vilaras, Christopoulos', in *Neos Ellinomnimon*, 13, 1916, 68–108.

———: 'I patris tou Rhiga' in *Neos Ellinomnimon*, 15, 1921, 53–80.

M. Laskaris: 'Opadoi tou Rhiga en Lipsai', in *Philologika Nea* (Kerkyra), I, 1945, 5–6.

S. Makraiou: 'Ypomnimata ekklisiastikis istorias (1750–1800)', in K. Sathas, *Mesaioniki Vivliothiki*, III (Venice 1872).

S. I. Mavromikhalos: 'I etaireia tou Rhiga kai t' apomnimonevmata tou Nik. Ypsilantou', in *Vivliophilia*, 6.3, 1952, 123–6.

A. J. Manessis: 'L'activité et les projets politiques d'un patriote Grec dans les Balkans vers la fin du XVIIIe siècle', in *Balkan Studies*, 3, 1962, 75–118.

U. de Marsillac: 'Esquisses biographiques—Rhigas', in *La voix de la Roumanie*, II, 1862.

Ph. Mikhalopoulos: 'O Rhigas kai oi Phanariotai', in *Nea Estia*, 43, 1948, 403–8.

A. Nikarousis: 'Pote o Mavroyenis proselave grammatea ton Rhigan?', in *Deltion tis istorikis kai ethnologikis etaireias* (new series), I, 1929, 53–88.

S. Nikolajević: 'Riga iz Phere', in *Otadzbina* (Belgrade), XXII, 1889, 104–22.

D. B. Oikonomidis: 'O Rhigas Pheraios en Vlakhiai', in *Athina*, 53, 1950, 130–146.

C. Papacostea-Danielopoulou: 'Les lectures grecques dans les Principautés Roumaines après 1821', in *Balkan Studies*, II, 1970, 157–68.

N. G. Politis: 'O Massaliotikos Thourios en Elladi', in *Parthenon*, II, 1872, 1089–93.

———: 'I neotis tou Rhiga', in *Estia*, 19.1, 1885, 13–16.

I. Rosenthal-Kamarinea: 'Einflüsse Kallinos' und Tyrtaios' auf den Thurios des Rigas', in *Folio Neohellenica*, 2, 1977, 127–36.

D. Stoikos: 'Viographia tou Rhiga tou Velestinli', in *Prometheus* (Volos), 7, 1894–5, 601 ff..

A. Svolos: 'Ta prota ellinika politevmata kai i epidrasis tis gallikis epanastaseos', in *Ephemeris ton ellinikon nomon*, II, 28–9, 1935, 737–9.

I. A. Thomopoulos: 'To protypo tou Scholeiou ton ntelikaton eraston', in *Nea Estia*, 48, 1950, 1028–38.

N. Traikoff: 'Rigas Velestinlis en Russie', in *Byzantinisch-neugriechische Jahrbücher*, 16, 1940, 156–68.

E. Vîrtosus: 'Nou despre Riga Velestinul, premergătorul independenţei greceşti', in *Revista Istorică*, 32, 1946, 92–114.

L. I. Vranousis: 'Agnosta patriotika phylladia kai anekdota keimena tis epokhis tou Rhiga kai tou Korai', in *Epeteris tou Mesaionikou archeiou*, 15–16, 1965–66.

C. M. Woodhouse: 'The Macedonian contribution to the struggle of Rhigas', in *Balkan Studies,* 30.1, 1989, 33–42.

D. Zakythinos: 'O Rhigas kai to orama tou oikonomikou kratous tis Anatolis', in *Eklogi,* 4, 1948, 170 ff..

P. G. Zerlentis: 'Patriarkhon grammata didaktika', in *Deltion tis istorikis kai ethnologikis etaireias* (new series), 9, 1977, 97–116.

G. T. Zoras: 'O Napoleon Bonapartis kai i synchroni elliniki poiisis', in *Nea Estia,* 1018, 1969, 1661–76.

VI BACKGROUND STUDIES

D. Alexandrakis: *Istoria tis Manis* (Athens 1902).

Anon.: *Briefe eines Augenzeugen der Griechischen Revolution vom Jahre 1821* (Halle 1824).

Anon. (? I. Kolettis): *Elliniki nomarkhia* (ed. G. Valetas, Athens 1949).

Anon. (Chr. Pamplekas): *Apantisis anonymou eis tous autou aphronas katigorous eponomasthisa peri Theokratias* (Leipzig 1793).

D. G. Apostolopoulos: *I galliki epanastasi stin tourkokratoumeni elliniki koinonia* (Athens 1989).

J. Baeyens: *Les Français à Corfou (1797–1799 et 1807–1814)* (Athens 1973).

J. J. Barthélemy: *Voyage du jeune Anacharsis en Grèce dans le milieu du quatrième siècle avant l'ère vulgaire* (7 vols., 2nd edition, Paris 1789).

A. Boppe: *L'Albanie et Napoléon, 1791–1814* (Paris 1914).

N. Botzaris: *Visions balkaniques dans la préparation de la révolution grecque, 1789–1821* (Geneva-Paris 1962).

C. A. Brandis: *Mittheilungen über Griechenland* (3 vols., Leipzig 1842).

A. Camariano-Cioran: *Les Académies princières de Bucarest et de Jassy et leurs professeurs* (Thessaloniki 1974).

R. M. Clogg: *The Movement for Greek Independence, 1770–1821* (London 1976).

—— (editor): *Balkan Society in the age of Greek Independence* (London 1981).

D. Dakin: *The Unification of Greece, 1770–1923* (London 1972).

R. Dalven: *Modern Greek Poetry* (New York 1949).

A. B. Daskalakis: *Meletai peri Rhiga Velestinli* (Athens 1964).

C. T. Dimaras: *La Grèce au temps des Lumières* (Geneva 1969).

——: *A History of Modern Greek Literature* (London 1974).

E. Driault: *La politique orientale de Napoléon* (Paris 1904).

J. C. von Engel: *Geschichte des Ungrischen Reichs und seiner Nebenländer* (4 vols., Halle 1797–1804).

C. Fauriel: *Chants populaires de la Grèce moderne* (Paris 1824).

É. Gaudin: *Du soulèvement des nations chrétiennes dans la Turquie européenne* (Paris 1822).

T. Gordon: *History of the Greek Revolution* (2 vols., London-Edinburgh, 1832).

G. F. Hertzberg: *Geschichte Griechenlands* (4 vols., Gotha 1879).

J. C. Hobhouse: *A Journey through Albania and other Provinces of Turkey in Europe and Asia to Constantinople during the Years 1809 and 1810* (2 vols., London 1813).

H. Holland: *Travels in the Ionian Isles, Albania, Thessaly etc., 1812 and 1813* (London 1815).

C. Iken: *Eunomia: Darstellungen und Fragmente neugriechischer Poesie und Prosa* (3 vols., Grimma 1827).

N. Iorga: *La Révolution française et le Sud-Est de l'Europe* (Bucharest 1934).

D. Kambouroglou: *Mémoires du Prince Nicolas Ypsilanti* (Athens 1901).

A. V. Kapsis: *O Rhigas Pheraios kai oi diekdikiseis tou ypodoulou Ellinismou kata ton 18 aiona* (Athens 1948).

P. Khiotis: *Logos viographikos peri Roma* (Athens 1857).

P. M. Kitromilides: *I galliki epanastasi kai i notioanatoliki Evropi* (Athens 1990).

———: *The Enlightenment as Social Criticism* (Princeton, 1992).

G. Konstantas and D. Philippidis: *Geographia neoteriki* (Vienna 1791).

A. Korais: *Adelphiki didaskalia* (Rome 1798; ed. G. Valetas, Athens 1949).

Y. Kordatos: *O Rhigas Pheraios kai i epokhi tou* (Athens 1931).

———: *O Rhigas Pheraios kai i valkaniki omospondia* (Athens 1974).

G. Laios: *O ellinikos typos tis Viennis apo tou 1784 mekhri tou 1821* (Athens 1961).

E. de las Cases: *Mémorial de Sainte-Hélène* (Paris 1961).

W. M. Leake: *Researches in Greece* (London 1814).

G. Lebel: *La France et les principautés danubiennes* (Paris 1855).

B. Lewis: *The Emergence of Modern Turkey* (Oxford 1968).

F. M. H. Markham: *Napoleon and the Awakening of Europe* (London 1961).

K. Melirroutos: *Chronologia istoriki* (Odessa 1838).

K. Nikolaidis: *Istoria tou Ellinismou* (Athens 1923).

A. Papadopoulos-Vretos: *Neoelliniki philologia* (Athens 1857).

C. Perrhaivos: *Istoria Souliou kai Pargas* (Venice 1815).

———: *Apomnimonevmata polemika* (ed. E. G. Protopsaltis, Athens 1956).

D. Petrakakos: *Koinovoulevtiki istoria tis Ellados* (Athens 1935).

I. Philemon: *Dokimion istorikon peri tis Philikis Etaireias* (Navplion 1834).

171

———: *Dokimion istorikon peri tis ellinikis epanastaseos* (4 vols., Athens 1859).

D. Photeinos: *Istoria tis palai Dakias* (3 vols., Vienna 1818).

D. Popovici: *La littérature roumaine à l'époque des Lumières* (Sibiu 1945).

F. C. H. L. Pouqueville: *Histoire de la régénération de la Grèce* (4 vols., Paris 1824).

F. C. H. L. Pouqueville: *Voyage dans la Grèce* (5 vols., Paris 1820–21).

M. Raybaud: *Mémoires sur la Grèce* (2 vols., Paris 1824–25).

I. Rizos-Neroulos: *Histoire moderne de la Grèce* (Geneva 1828).

———: *Cours de la littérature grecque moderne* (Geneva 1841).

D. Russo: *Studii istorice greco-româno* (2 vols., Bucharest 1939).

K. Sathas: *Mesaioniki Vivliothiki*, III (Venice 1872).

D. and N. Stephanopoli: *Voyage . . . en Grèce pendant les années 1797 et 1798* (2 vols., London 1800).

D. Szilagyi: *Jakobiner in der Habsburger-Monarchie* (Vienna 1962).

C. Trypanis: *Medieval and Modern Greek Poetry* (Oxford 1951).

A. F. Villemain: *Essai historique sur l'état des Grecs* (Paris 1825).

E. de Villeneuve: *Journal fait en Grèce pendant les années 1825 et 1826* (Brussels 1827).

M. Vovelle (editor): *L'Image de la Révolution française* (Paris-Oxford 1989).

L. I. Vranousis: *Les Chansons Phanariotes* (Athens 1970).

E. Wagermann: *From Joseph II to the Jacobin Trials* (Oxford 1959).

A. D. Xénopol: *Histoire des Roumains de la Dacie Trajane* (2 vols., Paris 1896).

S. T. Xenos: *I kivdileia itoi mia alithis istoria ton imeron mas* (London 1859).

G. I. Zaviras: *Nea Ellas, i ellinikon theatron* (ed. G. R. Kremos, Athens 1872).

A. Zub (editor): *La Révolution française et les Roumains* (Yassy 1989).

INDEX

account of Rhigas's early years, 7, 14, 16–17, 21–3, 25–7
first personal contacts with Rhigas, 48–50, 64–6, 81–3
on Rhigas's relations with Pasvanoglou, 21–3, 25–7, 90–1, 146–7
on secret societies (*hetairiai*), 23–6, 81–3, 95–6, 100
his own verses, 65–6
accompanies Rhigas to Trieste, 111, 113–18
deludes Austrian authorities, 116–19, 129–30
rumours of Rhigas's treatment under arrest, 118, 124
escapes to Corfu and abroad, 129–30, 153
on last days of Rhigas, 138, 147–8
publishes Rhigas's poems, 153
his later years, 150, 153, 156, 157
Pest, 49, 83, 86, 131
Peters, Kaspar, 47, 83, 93, 102, 132, 140
Petrovits, Philippos, 83, 92, 95–6, 101–3, 111, 119, 132, 137, 140
'Petonki', Baron, *see* Pittoni
Pherai (Velestino) 1, 38, 57
Pheraios (occasional name substituted for Velestinlis), *see* Rhigas
Philemon, 66, 114, 156
Philiki hetairia, 154–6
Philippides, Daniel, 18, 112
Photiadis, Lambros, 18, 87
Pichler press, 55
Pilizakis, 55
Pittoni, Count, 114–16, 118, 123
Plastaras, Nicholas, 48, 84, 114
Plato, 108
Politis, N. G., 158
Polyeidis, Theoklitos, 40
Polyzos (or Polyzois or Polyzoidis), N., 50, 61, 85, 87, 94, 96, 99, 120, 122, 131–2, 152
Potamos, 105
Potsa, Moukhoudar, 89
Poulios, George Markidis, 37–8, 47, 51, 72, 83, 87, 92, 94, 96, 111,

120, 127, 129, 137, 140, 146
Poulios, Publius Markidis, 37, 47, 51, 87, 94, 96
Poulios press, 37–8, 47, 51, 55, 57, 63–4, 110, 120, 123, 127, 129, 140
Preveza, 49, 88, 100, 107, 114, 118
Pringos, Ioannis, 3
Proclus, 3
Psalidas, Athanasios, 40, 90, 112
Ptolemy, 59–60

Rastadt, 107
Rathkeal, Baron von Herbert– , 37, 47, 84, 87, 94, 127–8, 132, 134–9, 141, 143–6, 148
Rétif de la Bretonne, 32–6, 44, 47, 160
Reis Effendi, 135; and *see* Attif Ahmed
Renner, J. B., 132
Rhigas Velestinlis (variously known as Antonios Zagoraios and Rhigas Pheraios)
date and place of birth, 1
name and cognomen (*see also* Kyritzis), 1, 3
childhood and schooldays, 1–4
departure from home for Constantinople, 5–9, 11–12
higher education, 3–4, 9, 18, 20, 31–6, 39, 45, 56–9, 112, 157, 162
attitude to classical/demotic Greek, 3–4, 19–20, 26, 32, 35, 70, 74–5, 150
service with Ypsilantis family, 13–14
service at Yassy and Bucharest, 14–15, 17–18, 20
commercial connections, 15, 20, 25, 39, 42, 45, 47–50, 55, 59, 88, 91–2, 135, 161
character and appearance, 15–19, 36, 61, 123–4, 157, 160–62
tastes and eccentricities, 17–18, 39, 50, 59, 93, 112–13
European sympathies, 15, 17–18, 23, 31, 43–5
experience of combat, 6–7, 11, 20–3, 27
understanding of Turks and Muslims, 22–6, 77–9

role in secret societies (*hetairiai*), 23–6, 79, 81–96, 100, 121, 146, 154–5

his personal seal, 25, 64, 75, 116

first visit to Vienna, 29–38

return to Bucharest, 38–9

second visit to Vienna, 50–62, 85–6, 96, 98–103, 130

other travels (verified or doubtful) in southern or western Europe, 39–40, 49–50, 115

religious faith, 22–6, 40–2, 73–4, 77–8, 111, 130, 154

feminist sentiment, 35–6, 70–1, 75–6

private and semi-official activities, 17, 27, 39, 44, 124, 130–1

revolutionary ambitions, 44–8, 50–1, 57–62, 70–1, 110, 121–3, 156, 162

plans for revolution, 63, 67–8, 86–96, 98–105, 107

attempts to launch revolution, 101–4, 110–15

betrayal, arrest and interrogation at Trieste, 114–19

attempted suicide, 123–4

transferred in chains to Vienna, 124–5, 130

last days in prison at Vienna, 127–41

extradited to Turkish authorities, 134, 140–1, 143

executed by Turks at Belgrade, 147–9

posthumous reputation, 149–62

Rhigas's works, by categories

Poems and songs

Thourios, 7, 24, 50, 58, 61, 64, 69, 76–9, 84–5, 90, 93, 99–100, 121, 128, 139, 141, 144, 153, 155, 162

Second *Thourios* ('Patriotic Hymn'), 65, 89, 153

Paean ('Greek Marseillaise', authorship doubtful), 45, 66–7, 153

Other verses, 35, 64–6, 153–4

Maps and drawings

Map of Hellas, 19, 38, 50–9, 63–4, 66, 78, 84, 92, 99–100, 111, 139, 157

Moldavia, 42, 55, 64, 111, 132, 152, 157

Vallachia, 42, 55, 64, 111, 157

Alexander the Great, 55, 59–60, 111, 140, 157

Translations

Barthélemy's *Anacharsis* (in part), 9, 51, 57, 93–4, 121–2, 139

Montesquieu's *Esprit des lois* (never completed), 32, 44

The Moral Tripod, 51, 55–7, 111, 121, 140; comprising:

Metastasio's *Olympia*, 51, 56–7, 111, 156, 159

Marmontel's *Shepherdess of the Alps*, 51, 56

Gessner's *First Sailor*, 51, 56

Educational works

Anthology of Physics, 31–3, 36, 38, 44

Other references, 20, 27, 46

Romances

School of Delicate Lovers, 31–7, 40, 44, 160

Love's Consequences (doubtfully attributed), 40

Religious texts

Prophecies of Agathangelos, 40–2

Other references, 68, 77–9, 156

Political writings

New Political Order 24, 63–4, 67–76, 85, 91–4, 110–11, 120–2, 130–1, 133, 140–1, 150, 155, 157–8, 160; including:

Proclamation, 68, 157

Rights of Man, 68–71, 76, 157, 159

Constitution, 71–6, 157, 159

Military Manual, 63–5, 67–8, 88, 98, 110–11, 129, 133, 160; including:

Concise Theory of Khevenhüller (summarised by Rhigas), 64–5, 160

Democratic Catechism (not extant), 65

Two songs imitating rhythm of French and German originals (*Carmagnole* and *Freut euch des Lebens*), 65–6

Rhine, River, 107
Robespierre, 44
Romania, 15, 17–18, 39, 58
Romas, Dionysios, 85, 89
Rouget de Lisle, 45
Roumeli, 64, 68, 89, 107, 111
Rousseau, Jean-Jacques, 34, 44, 57
Ruschuk, 136

St Helena, 107–8
St Just, 44
Sakellarios, George, 57, 96, 154
Saumil, Baron von, 130
Sava, River, 58
Schertz, Colonel, 147–8
Seleucus, 59–60
Semlin (Zemun), 49, 86, 100, 143
Serbia, 91–2, 108, 136
Sevastos, Markos, 61, 85
Siatista, 83, 100
Sieyès, Abbé, 44, 101–3
Simonides, 57
Sištov, Treaty of, 43
Slatineanu, Iordache, 17, 87
Smith, Sidney, 108
Smyrna, 49, 55, 84, 91–2, 122, 139, 150
Solon, 71, 93
Sophocles, ix, 57
Souli, 68, 89, 110
Soutzos, Michael, 39–40, 43–4, 78, 84
Stageira, 59
Stamatis (Stamaty), Constantine, 18, 43–4, 105
Steiger (or Stinger), Elias, 102
Stephanopoli, Dimo, 105–8
Stephanopoli, Nicolo, 105–8
Stephen, St, 160

Talleyrand, Comte, 105
Tempe, Vale of, 104
Theocharis, George, 39, 83, 96, 118, 120–1, 152
Thermopylai, 57
Thessaly, 1–2, 5, 8–9, 26, 49–50, 57, 73, 82–3, 88–9, 96, 104, 112, 130, 155, 157
Thiersch, Friedrich, 157

Thrace, 26, 106
Thucydides, 4
Thugut, Baron, 127, 134–9, 141, 143–5
Thurn, Baron, 118
Torountzias, George, 86
Torountzias, Theocharis, 82, 86, 96, 100, 110, 121, 131
Toullios, Constantine, 83, 86–7, 131
Toulon, 148
Tournavitis, Dimitrakis, 29, 43, 48, 87, 137
Tournavitis, Michael, 48, 84, 87, 137
Trattner press, 36–7
Trieste, 1, 25, 31, 39, 47, 49–50, 55–6, 71–2, 82–5, 88, 92, 98, 100–1, 110–11, 114–18, 122–4, 129, 133, 135, 137, 140
Typaldos, Constantine, 152
Typaldos, Julius, 157
Tzoumerka, 89

Ukraine, 79
Ushakov, Admiral, 117

Vallachia, 13, 15, 20–1, 29, 42, 51, 55, 58–9, 64, 87–8, 102, 105, 111, 130, 136, 157
Vasileiou, Alexander, 92
Vatopedi monastery, 7, 12
Velestinlis, see Rhigas
Velestino, 1–2, 4–6, 8–9, 157
Vendotis, George, 37–8, 40, 57, 85
Venice, 62, 72, 84–5, 98, 100, 104, 106, 110, 113–14
Verona, 62
Vidin, 11, 21–3, 37, 147
Vienna, 18, 22, 27, 29–32, 47, 49–51, 55–6, 58–9, 61–2, 63, 71, 78, 82–3, 85–8, 96, 98–103, 106, 110, 113–15, 117–18, 122–5, 130–6, 143–4, 152–4, 158–60
Vilaras, Ioannis, 85
Villestindis (corruption of Velestinlis), 1, 130
Vlachavas, 89
Vlachobogdania, 64, 68
Vlastos, see Mesinezis,

Volos, 1, 5, 157
Voltaire, 34
Vostitsa, *see* Aigion
Voulgaris, Evgenios, 112, 154, 157

Wallenburg, 135, 144–5
Warsaw, 44
Westphalia, 83

Yassy, 13–15, 18–19, 44, 49, 55, 87,
 94, 122, 131–2, 153–4
Yassy, Treaty of, 43
Ypsilantis, Alexander (1726–1806), 8,
 12–15, 20, 23, 143
Ypsilantis, Alexander (1792–1828), 12,
 47, 55, 154
Ypsilantis, Constantine (c. 1760–1816),
 13, 47, 127, 135, 143–6, 155

Ypsilantis, Dimitrios (1793–1832),
 12–13, 155
Ypsilantis, Dimitrios (brother of
 Constantine), 13
Ypsilantis, Nicholas, 12, 24–5, 76, 81,
 96, 155

Zagora, 1–4, 130
Zagoraios, Antonios (pseudonym of
 Rhigas), 1, 3
Zakharias, 89
Zakynthos, 37, 85, 104–5, 157
Zalokostas, George, 5, 157
Zambelias, I., 156
Zaviras, George, 151
'Zeloprophitis', 40–1
Ziras, Spyro, 6–7, 89
Zitsa, 82

THE ROMIOSYNI SERIES
Studies and translations in the field
of modern Greek culture

❄

The Marble Threshing Floor: Studies in Modern Greek Poetry
by Philip Sherrard

A Greek Quintet: Poems by Cavafy, Sikelianos, Seferis, Elytis, Gatsos
selected and translated by Edmund Keeley and Philip Sherrard

The Isles of Greece & Other Poems
by Demetrios Capetanakis, with an introduction by Edith Sitwell

Dionysius Solomos
by Romilly Jenkins

On the Greek Style: Selected Essays on Poetry and Hellenism
translated by Rex Warner and Th. D. Frangopoulos
with an introduction by Rex Warner

The Mind & Art of C. P. Cavafy: Essays on his Life and Work
by E. M. Forster, Patrick Leigh Fermor, Robert Liddell,
George Seferis, Stephen Spender and others

Edward Lear: The Cretan Journal
edited and with an introduction by Rowena Fowler

The Pursuit of Greece
an anthology selected and introduced by Philip Sherrard
with photographs by Dimitri

Fair Greece: Sad Relic: Literary Philhellenism from Shakespeare to Byron
by Terence Spencer

Edward Lear: The Corfu Years
a chronicle presented through Lear's letters and journals
edited and with an introduction by Philip Sherrard

Road to Rembetika: Music of a Greek Sub-culture
by Gail Holst

The Greek East and the Latin West: A Study in the Christian Tradition
by Philip Sherrard

Portrait of a Greek Mountain Village
by Juliet du Boulay

❄

DENISE HARVEY (PUBLISHER), 340 05 LIMNI, EVIA, GREECE